THE PSYCHOLOGY
OF GENDER

What is the difference between sex and gender? What is the impact of gender-role stereotypes on our lives, our relationships and the world? What does gender mean to you?

The Psychology of Gender looks at our biology, history and culture to consider the impact of gender roles and stereotypes, and addresses the 'dilemmas' we have regarding gender in a post-modern world. It offers a unique perspective on gender through storytelling and explores ideas around transgender and cisgender identities and androgyny, tackling hidden assumptions and helping us make sense of the world of gender.

By examining the future of gender, *The Psychology of Gender* offers a platform for further exploration, and arrives at a new psychology of gender that emphasises relationships and helps us to understand our own gender identity and that of those around us.

Dr Gary W. Wood is a Chartered Psychologist, Solution-Focused Coach, advice columnist and teacher. He has taught psychology and research methods at several UK universities and is regularly featured in the media.

THE PSYCHOLOGY OF EVERYTHING

The Psychology of Everything is a series of books which debunk the myths and pseudo-science surrounding some of life's biggest questions.

The series explores the hidden psychological factors that drive us, from our sub-conscious desires and aversions, to the innate social instincts handed to us across the generations. Accessible, informative, and always intriguing, each book is written by an expert in the field, examining how research-based knowledge compares with popular wisdom, and illustrating the potential of psychology to enrich our understanding of humanity and modern life.

Applying a psychological lens to an array of topics and contemporary concerns – from sex to addiction to conspiracy theories – The Psychology of Everything will make you look at everything in a new way.

Titles in the series:

For further information about this series please visit www.thepsychologyofeverything.co.uk

THE
PSYCHOLOGY
OF GENDER

GARY W. WOOD

Routledge
Taylor & Francis Group

LONDON AND NEW YORK

First published 2018
by Routledge
2 Park Square, Milton Park, Abingdon, Oxon OX14 4RN

and by Routledge
711 Third Avenue, New York, NY 10017

Routledge is an imprint of the Taylor & Francis Group, an informa business

British Library Cataloguing-in-Publication Data
A catalogue record for this book is available from the British Library

Library of Congress Cataloging-in-Publication Data
A catalog record for this title has been requested

ISBN: 978-1-138-74839-2 (hbk)
ISBN: 978-1-138-74857-6 (pbk)
ISBN: 978-1-315-18022-9 (ebk)

Typeset in Joanna
by Apex CoVantage, LLC

MIX
Paper from
responsible sources
FSC   FSC® C013604   Printed and bound by CPI Group (UK) Ltd, Croydon, CR0 4YY
www.fsc.org

CONTENTS

ACKNOWLEDGEMENTS

Thanks to everyone who supported the writing process, especially Eleanor Reedy at Routledge for her patience, support and constructive suggestions. Thanks also to Alex Howard and the rest of the team, and to Christine Cottone and the team at Apex CoVantage. Many thanks to Sarah Baxter and The Society of Authors for support in the completion of this book.

Special thanks to Petra Boynton for her support over the years, and for always 'putting my name forward'.

Very special thanks to Takeshi Fujisawa for his moral and technical support, and patience.

Dedicated to Nelly Florence Butcher and Clifford Bertram Butcher.

1

INTRODUCTION

Welcome to *The Psychology of Gender* in which we explore the implications of our classification, at birth, of 'boy' or 'girl' and how it impacts on all aspects of our lives.

CONVENTIONAL WISDOM ABOUT GENDER

We hear people say, in times of extreme stress or near-death experiences, 'my whole life flashed before me'. However, what if, in a moment of precognition, our lives did flash before us at our very first breath? What if all the twists and turns, the patterns and choices were pre-determined? What if one flick of the pen mapped out our whole lives, based on a cursory glance of our infant nakedness? What if the 'lottery of our anatomy' was our destiny and biology and physiology determined our psychology? It sounds like a sinister plot from a dystopian science fiction novel.[1] And yet, every day, from every tick on a form we make to every bathroom break we take, we confirm and reconfirm our birth identities in pretty much this way: from girls and boys, to males and females, to ladies and gentlemen.

The Psychology of Gender is a short volume in The Psychology of Everything series offering a critical introduction aiming to bridge the gaps between everyday understanding, pop-psychology and academic writing. Everyday understanding harbours many taken-for-granted assumptions, and pop-psychology, with its comedic metaphors, aims to soothe and simplify – obscuring more than it illuminates. Although academia aims to shine a light on the unexplored, it sometimes over-intellectualizes so that it feels divorced from everyday reality. Sociologist Ken Plummer describes gender as 'the surest of all ideas in the modern world and at the same time one of the most contested concepts in the social sciences'.[2] This book aims to tackle the key hidden assumptions surrounding gender, answer some questions, stimulate your own questions and guide further exploration.

Gender 'hides in plain sight'. Psychologist Vivien Burr describes it as 'the backcloth against which our daily lives are played out'.[3] Gender is the 'arena in which we face hard practical issues about justice, identity and even survival'.[4] However, it is often treated as little more than 'an interesting personality trait'. From my experience of teaching research methods, students routinely include 'gender differences' in their projects without questioning if it makes sense. Pop-psychology upholds this view, by encouraging us to think of men and women as so different that they are from different planets. Academic psychology has been slow to challenge this, as social psychologist Mary Crawford contends that the Mars/Venus books and workshops gained legitimacy through advertising in academic journals.[5] Throughout the 1990s LGBTQ[6] writers increasingly challenged the 'taken-for-grantedness' of gender. In *The Apartheid of Sex: A Manifesto on the Freedom of Gender*,[7] Martine Rothblatt compares the challenges to the binary gender paradigm with heretical challenges to the earth-centred paradigm of the universe.

Before we continue, think about the last time you completed an official form. Declarations of sex or gender on such forms traditionally offered two options:

- Are you male?
- Are you female?

It never occurred to many people that it could be anything other than 'either/or'. Then one day the forms changed, offering options such as 'other' and 'prefer not to say'. Some would decry these changes as an assault on the 'natural order' or 'political correctness gone mad'. Why would anyone *prefer* not to say? What else could there be beyond male and female? Others welcomed the opportunity of alternatives to the binary gender labels that better captured the reality of their lives. *The Psychology of Gender* aims to address these issues and more besides. Once you dare to question gender, the questions write themselves.

Why are the 'helpers' in artificial intelligence (AI) applications feminized (e.g. Siri, Cortana) when they do not need to be? Why are sports not organized by body size instead of gender? Are gender stereotypes bad for our health? Are gender roles a benign way of organizing the world? What is the connection between gender, power and inequality? Do self-help books offer the solutions to take us forward or sticking plasters for the status quo? Are gender differences hardwired in the brain? Is there more to you than pink or blue? Can we exist in a world without gender, or is resistance futile?

So where do we begin?

In academic psychology, it is a convention to start by clarifying the terms of the debate – brief, working definitions, so we are all, so to speak, on the same page. What is psychology? What is gender? What's the connection between sex and gender?

WHAT IS PSYCHOLOGY?

The accepted definition of psychology is 'the scientific study of mind and behaviour'.[8] It adopts scientific methods (like the natural sciences) to explore, in a systematic way, what it means to be human and what makes us tick. Methods include controlled experiments, observations, surveys and so on. The aim is to generate data, in the form of numbers (quantitative) or words and pictures (qualitative) or a combination. Researchers in psychology analyze these data to test research questions, generate explanations, develop and refine theories, generalize and make predictions of future behaviours. Psychology offers a means to test the assumptions of everyday understanding (and pop-psychology). Sometimes it confirms 'common sense', and at other times it offers a radically different view.

Psychology is not infallible, as research can never be conducted in a 'values vacuum'. It is vulnerable to errors and biases that inevitably creep in when people study people.[9] Psychology is a work in progress, and part of its project is to make visible the invisible and expose human bias in ever increasing approximations to 'the truth'. It offers an alternative to the phrase that irked many an inquisitive child at school: 'because that's just the way things are'.

As a personal and professional development coach, I use the principle with clients that 'the viewing influences the doing, and vice versa'. How we view the world influences what we do in the world. Sex and gender, as fundamental units of identity, create lenses (or filters) through which we interact with the world, influencing how we think, how we behave and experience the world and ourselves as part of it.

WHAT IS GENDER (AND HOW DOES IT RELATE TO SEX)?

Sex and gender are often used interchangeably, giving the impression that they are different words for expressing the same thing. In everyday language, some use gender as though it is a more polite alternative to saying 'sex', rather like using euphemisms for 'toilet', such as restroom, powder room, little boys' room and the loo. Sex and gender are interrelated, but they are not synonymous. The tendency to blend and blur the terms can colour our thinking and obscure the fundamental differences. It makes it easier for us to assume that gender is a natural and inevitable product of our biology when it isn't.

Sex has two meanings: a physical activity or a biological status. The act of having (or doing) sex is to engage in physical/genital intimacy with another person or persons, or of any self-stimulation, and not excluding inanimate objects.[10] Sex as part of our identity – a state of being – is usually allocated at birth, primarily based on the appearance of our genitals. Mainly, it is an either/or binary classification of boy or girl which appears on our birth certificates. This sets in motion a series of expectations for the rest of our lives – that is, our gender.[11]

Gender is the sociocultural (and psychological) interpretation of our biological sex, that is, how we make sense of the biology in everyday life. Whereas 'male' and 'female' are biological distinctions, 'masculine' and 'feminine' are gender distinctions. According to the hard-line view, masculinity results from maleness and femininity results from femaleness. This book aims to explore the grey areas, beyond this broad assumption, including whether sex and gender can be 'divorced' from one another. To begin questioning this, it helps to think of sex as a noun (something we are) and gender as the verb (something we do).

WHAT TO EXPECT FROM THIS BOOK

The Psychology of Gender draws on a wealth of theories and evidence from a broad review of disciplines to consider the impact of gender on our individual and collective psychologies, including our relationships and society in general. This short book cannot possibly offer an exhaustive examination, but rather highlights key themes and issues to offer a springboard for further critical reading. Gender is found in biology, sociology, physiology, social geography, queer theory, LGBTQI+ writing, feminist writing, cognitive neuroscience, cultural studies and so on. All inform and impact on our psychology. I also draw on my own research, which explains homophobia in terms of gender-role transgression, making explicit the link between homophobia and sexism. By a critical examination of the evidence, hopefully, we can arrive at a new psychology of gender, one that is less prescriptive and more meaningfully descriptive. One that draws parallels between future models of gender and models from cross-cultural and historical perspectives. One that considers the psychological complexity of the human experience.

- Chapter 2 considers the distinctions between sex and gender in greater depth, discusses gender roles and their relationship to our anatomy and how neither biological sex nor socialized gender is necessarily binary. It also considers the links between gender identity and having (or doing) sex.
- What does the research say about biological sex differences and 'gendered brains', their links to gender-role stereotypes and how they are interpreted and reported in pop-psychology circles? Chapter 3 takes a more in-depth look at the basis of perceived differences in gender.
- Are gender roles a benign way of organizing the world? The 'equal but different' view of gender often ignores the power relations (and inequalities). Chapter 4 considers the impact of enforcing gender-role stereotypes, including the individual psychological and health implications, the impact on friendships, relationships and society.
- Chapter 5 considers alternative stories for making sense of gender, other than the modern-day Western binary perspective that inhabits pop-psychology books. It considers where the story started and other world views as well as fairy tales, science fiction and cyber identities to help us begin to formulate a new blueprint for the psychology of gender.

Our journey through the psychology of gender concludes by drawing together the main themes and asking you to consider how the information impacts on you. What has struck a chord with you or struck fear into your heart? How will you make sense of it in relation to your understanding of yourself? How would you describe a gender that is meaningful to your life? What's your story?

So, let's begin by going back to basics and exploring the links between sex and gender.

2

SEX AND GENDER

TWO ROADS?

Debates around gender invariably centre on the assumed 'naturalness' of gender roles, that they are 'hardwired' and an inevitable result of our biology – that is, penises lead to masculinity and vaginas lead to femininity. This leads us to think of the body as 'a kind of machine that manufactures gender difference'.[1] From this perspective, the road is well travelled, and the route is predestined. In contrast, Judith Butler in *Gender Trouble* describes gender as a practice, as something we do. It is 'the repeated stylization of the body, a set of repeated acts within a highly rigid regulatory frame that congeal over time to produce the appearance of substance, of a natural sort of being'.[2] On this view, it is about performance rather than essence, with 'the body as a kind of canvas on which culture paints images of gender'.[3] It 'boils down' to the age-old nature versus nurture debate with which every psychology student must wrangle.

Building on the basic definitions offered in the introduction, this chapter first goes back to basics to review biological sex and the extent to which everything 'lines up'. Is there a coherent binary narrative or 'shades of grey' and ambiguity? In developing the definition of gender, it introduces the idea that we interpret sex and gender through a set of lenses. The chapter also discusses intersex, transgender and cisgender and, finally, considers the relationship between gender and sexuality (sexual orientation).

THE LENSES OF GENDER

In the 1990s, to unearth the hidden assumptions about gender differences, psychologist Sandra Bem proposed three lenses with which we view gender: *biological essentialism, androcentrism,* and *gender polarization*.[4] These offer a starting point for a critical appraisal of sex and gender narratives in common understanding, pop-psychology and academia.

Biological essentialism puts our focus on differences in reproductive biology as the primary signifier of gender difference. The genitals become the 'passports to gender'. In the popular imagination reproductive biology offers a fixed blueprint for the way men and women make sense of the world, themselves and relationships. Gender theorist and performer Kate Bornstein describes pop-psychology's Mars/Venus approach as 'quick-fix essentialism' (which only works if we accept the first premise).[5] *Androcentrism* literally means 'male-centred'.[6] Through this lens, masculinity is given precedence over femininity. *Gender polarization* renders masculinity and femininity as binary opposites, one being expressed at the expense of the other – a zero-sum game. We reaffirm this every time we use the terms 'opposite sex' and 'battle of the sexes'. On this view, behaviours crossing gender lines are treated as a joke or even pathology.[7] Bem argues that the lenses interact not only to create a coherent view of the world, but also to separate men and women unequally (sexism). Rather than merely helping to explain the world, they distort our view. To test Bem's thesis, let's re-examine human biology, which – as scientific 'facts' – should be insusceptible to the gender lenses.

SEX IS IN THE EYE OF THE BEHOLDER

Reproductive anatomy

Sex is usually assigned at birth by sight on the presence or absence of a penis. It is not particularly scientific but, nevertheless, that is what happens. Although pretty important, for many people, genital shape is only a partial definition of sex. Biological sex is also defined by chromosomes, hormones, the function of the reproductive system and the sex of the internal accessory organs – the embryonic forerunners of the reproductive structures.[8] Most often they all line up, but there is not always a perfect correlation. Let's first consider the function and outward appearance of our genitals, including gonads (ovaries/testes), which for males are also external (see Table 2.1).

Table 2.1 Comparison of female and male genitalia

Female	Male
ovaries	testes
labia majora (outer lips)	scrotum
labia minora (inner lips)	underside of penis
glans (head) of the clitoris	glans (head) of penis
shaft (erectile tissue) of the clitoris	corpus cavernosum (erectile tissue)
vagina	*no comparable structure*

Comparing structures in Table 2.1, when located side-by-side they are formed from the same embryonic tissue. The main difference is greater visibility of male genitalia compared with female genitalia. Female gonads (ovaries) are also internal. However, there are strong similarities between the two configurations, with one notable exception. Males do not have any structure that resembles a vagina, except for a feint trace where scrotal swellings fused together. Although 'vagina' is used routinely for female genitalia, the vagina is only the birth canal, thus putting emphasis on reproduction – a case of biological essentialism. Correctly speaking, the collective term is vulva[9] (although *The Vulva Monologues* doesn't have quite the same ring to it). Shifting the focus to sexual pleasure, the penis and the clitoris are natural complements. Notably, the clitoris, not adequately researched until the 1990s is the only organ in the human body with the sole function of sexual pleasure. In her film *Viva la Vulva: Women's Sex Organs Revealed*, pro-sex feminist and pioneering educator Betty Dodson teaches that most of the clitoris is subterranean, so Table 2.1 needs a radical revision to include the internal clitoris. And yet in common understanding, it is routinely described as a 'miniature penis' – an example of androcentrism.[10] Later in the chapter, we examine, further, the primacy of the penis. Meanwhile, we take a brief detour to consider other parts of the anatomy common to all.

Other anatomy

Although many parts of our anatomy have no reproductive purpose they might still fulfil an erotic one. Males and females have five senses (sight, hearing, touch, taste and smell) in common. Also, mouths have identical physiology and function, as do hands, although on average men's hands are larger.

Undoubtedly the body part that is the source of greatest contention is the anus, a topic for which it is hard to be neutral. It has become a symbol of dirtiness,[11] and anal stimulation is considered by some people to be a wilful perversion of the 'natural sexual urge'. Biologically, the anus is common to both sexes and shares muscles and a nervous structure with its neighbour, the genitals. It has an erotic potential for everyone, irrespective of sexual orientation.[12] However, attitudes to the anus are divided along gender lines. In an experiment, participants were asked to rate all aspects of the human body on several scales. Results showed that overall the female anus was rated more 'sexual', 'attractive' and 'positive' in comparison to the male anus. Comparing the scores by the gender of the participants, the attitudes of females appeared more objective, that is, more closely aligned with biological reality. By contrast, male participants overestimated the sexual capacity of the female anus and underestimated the sexual capacity of the male anus – overemphasizing the permeability of the female body and underplaying the permeability of the male. From an androcentric perspective, the female anus is a surrogate vagina, while the male anus is always off-limits. Similar gender differences in attitudes were observed for ratings of the mouth and hands. All three gender lenses are operating here.[13]

Let's now go right back to basics and consider our chromosomes.

CHROMOSOMAL SEX

The platform

Genes are the units of heredity (such as the colour of eyes and facial shape) passed down from parents to their offspring. Chromosomes are long, stringy coiled packets of genes that carry this heredity information. Human genes are encoded on 23 pairs of chromosomes (46 in all). For females, all chromosomes are X-shaped. For males, one item in the last pair is Y-shaped (so called because it appears to have one branch of the X missing). This difference determines the genetic sex of the embryo. For a female, the 23rd chromosome is XX, and for a male it is XY. The first item in the pair (X) comes from the egg of the mother. The father's sperm produces the difference in the second chromosome in the pair. So, an 'X sperm' produces XX (girl), and a 'Y sperm' produces XY (boy). The Y chromosome has some of the genes missing of the X chromosome, which does not protect the male so well from hereditary diseases. For a female, an atypical gene from both parents is required to cause disease; it needs to affect both X chromosomes. For the male, there is only one X to affect. From a chromosomal perspective, then, *males* are the more vulnerable (weaker) sex,[14] contradicting the traditional (androcentric) view.

According to Sadie Plant in *Zeros and Ones*,[15] the two basic prototypes for human beings are, mainly, double female (XX) or half-female/half-male (XY) with the 'egg' as the default and the sperm producing the variation. Although there are many variations on these prototypes (with extra X and Y chromosomes), it is not possible to have YY, although there can be an XYY and an XXX. It is even possible to have a single X (X0), but never a single Y. The X from the egg always forms the primary platform. Thus, chromosomal sex challenges the primacy given to maleness. Chromosomal variations are discussed further later in this chapter in the section on people with intersex conditions.

Chromosomes and genitals

Once fertilized, the egg divides to produce more cells. Regardless of the chromosome carried by the sperm, the genitals of the embryo are indistinct until about the seventh or eighth week, and even after that it takes a trained eye to tell the difference. At around three months hormone activity triggers more marked changes. With an XY (male) embryo, two main hormones are produced. One stimulates the development of the male reproductive system and another inhibits the development of the female reproductive system (causing it to recede). By contrast, for the XX (female) embryo, there is relatively little hormone production; nevertheless, the female reproductive system develops. The embryo may be XY, but if the hormones do not trigger changes at the crucial time and in the appropriate amounts, the embryo will develop, automatically, along the female route. Biology will produce a female unless given instructions to the contrary. So, if being pedantic, it is more accurate to describe the penis as an enlarged clitoris. From three months onwards, embryonic tissue typically takes different routes (female or male), as shown in Table 2.1.

As our hormones are cited as the agents of difference in genital development we take a closer look at these next.

HORMONAL SEX

Hormones are chemical messengers produced by glands in the body. Circulating in the bloodstream, hormones control the actions of cells and organs, that is, they switch bodily processes on and off. They are often regarded as the 'bad guys' of biology and implicated in negative aspects of behaviour such as mood swings, irrationality and acts of aggression (all partly true). We don't know, exactly, how many hormones are in the human body – it could run into the hundreds.[16] However, discussions invariably focus on the few we call male hormones and female hormones. Although, suspiciously, the term 'hormonal' seems only to apply to women, and usually in a negative way. When comparing biological sex, hormones differ more by degree than by type. The number and range of hormones produced by males and females are virtually the same. Usually referred to as sex hormones, although they serve other functions in the body, females produce a preponderance of *oestrogen* and *progesterone*, whereas males produce a preponderance of *androgens* (notably, *testosterone*).

Testosterone, produced in the gonads (testes and ovaries) and the adrenal glands, helps with the regulation of the sex drives of both men and women, but also with fat distribution, muscle bulk, energy and a sense of well-being. The average amount of testosterone differs between males and females, but both have it. Thinking of progesterone only as a female hormone obscures many of its functions, such as helping to build and maintain bone mass. Progesterone is also the precursor to testosterone and oestrogen. It is an anti-depressant, it aids in blood clotting, helps to regulate brain activity, contributes to the initiation of sleep, contributes to the process that converts fat into energy, can assist in 'rebooting' the libido (sex drive) and more besides.[17] Sex differences relate to differing, average proportions of hormones rather than absolute differences. The patterns and proportions of hormones vary substantially within the sexes, not just between them. Furthermore, rather than two sets of hormones operating separately, there are extensive interactions (cooperation) between them.

Overall, in typical development, there is no such thing as 100% female ('all woman') or 100% male ('all man') in biological terms.[18] The picture of sex development is not complete without considering variations from the binary theme.

INTERSEX – VARIATIONS OF REPRODUCTIVE/SEX DEVELOPMENT

For intersex conditions, there is not a total correlation between all partial definitions of sex. Reproductive or sexual anatomy and/or chromosome pattern and/or hormonal activity do not fit standardized definitions of biological maleness or femaleness. From a review of international medical literature from 1955 to 1998, researchers concluded that it might be as high as 2% of live births. The frequency of individuals receiving 'corrective' genital surgery, however, runs between one and two per 1000 live births (0.1 to 0.2%).[19]

The UK Intersex Association (UKIA) advocates the use of 'intersex' as a collective term, although it recognizes that not all people with such conditions are comfortable with the term. However, there are stronger objections to alternative terminology proposed by the International Consensus Conference on Intersex held in the USA in 2005. Despite the word 'consensus', the conference had an almost exclusive medical emphasis and its attempt to devise a more suitable term for intersex resulted in *disorders of sex development* (DSD). Given changes in attitudes and approaches to gay people and trans people (moving away from the language of disorder), this seems a retrograde step. UKIA argues that there was very little input from people with intersex conditions and the use of 'disorder' stigmatizes 'natural variations in human development'. Consequently, it reduces the lives of people (with individual identities and histories) to 'disorders' that need to be managed. UKIA offers two less stigmatizing alternatives for use by the medical profession: *variations in sex development* or *variations in reproductive development*.[20]

The following figures are given to illustrate that intersex conditions are not as rare as we might think. However, it's vital to remember that behind the statistics are individual stories that can only enrich our understanding of the psychology of sex and gender. As it stands, currently, there is a marked shortfall in this knowledge.

Chromosomal variations

The most common variation on the XX–XY theme is *Klinefelter syndrome* (KS) occurring in one in around 1000 live births. It results from two or more X chromosomes in males (e.g. XXY). The condition is random and not inherited from the parents. The outward indicators of KS may be subtle in many cases. The primary feature is infertility and sometimes hindered genital development. In around one in 3000 live births are females who have only one X chromosome that is fully functional (X0) – a random condition, that is not inherited, known as *Turner syndrome* (TS). Indicators associated with TS vary among women. Menstruation can be delayed but remedied with hormone therapy, and fertility issues addressed with IVF treatment.

Hormonal variations

Androgen Insensitivity Syndrome (AIS) occurs where the development of male chromosomes (XY) shows resistance to androgens, resulting in a person with some or all the physical traits of a female. AIS can be full (complete) or partial. It is the outcome of an inherited genetic effect located on the X chromosome. Complete androgen insensitivity prevents the penis and other male body parts from developing, so, at birth, the baby appears female. Secondary sex characteristics occur at puberty (such as breasts), but without a uterus they will not menstruate. Full AIS, accounting for one in 13,000 live births, is not usually noticed until puberty, whereas partial AIS, accounting for one in 130,000 live births, is more probably seen at birth.

The most common of all conditions is *Congenital Adrenal Hyperplasia* (CAH), a group of inherited conditions that are present at birth where the adrenal glands (on top of the kidneys) are larger than usual. In CAH, the body is missing an enzyme that stimulates the adrenal glands to release the cortisol hormone, meaning the body is less able to cope with stress, either emotionally or physically. In the more severe cases of CAH, boys show indications soon after birth, when they develop heart rhythm irregularities. For females born with severe CAH, there might be uncertainty about the sex of the baby because of ambiguous or male-looking genitalia. Puberty tends to be on the earlier side for girls and boys and both tend to have voices deeper than average. In girls, periods are irregular or absent. Boys tend to have an enlarged penis and smaller (than average) testicles. Classical CAH occurs in about one in 13,000 births.

Late-onset CAH (also called Non-classical CAH) is a milder form of CAH manifesting in later childhood or even young adulthood. It can account for up to one in 66 people in some ethnic groups. It is not characterized by ambiguous genitalia in girls and does not lead to full CAH. For some with late-onset CAH, there are no notable indications, and the condition is only identified because a relative has sought medical attention for issues related to the condition (such as unwanted body hair, irregular menstruation or severe acne). For many, issues resulting from non-classical CAH are treatable with very low-dose steroids, and this does not necessarily have to be lifelong.[21]

Gonadal variations

In about one in 83,000 live births, newborns have gonads known as *ovotestes*. These, as the name suggests, contain both ovarian and testicular tissue. These might be instead of one or both ovaries or testes. The condition was formerly known as true hermaphroditism but it does not necessarily indicate what external genitalia will look like, which may be somewhat typical of either sex or something in-between. Testicular tissue in ovotestes has an increased risk of cancer, and so this portion is often removed or monitored closely.

This chapter does not represent a complete review of all intersex conditions; however, it does show that a belief in absolute biological binaries of sex is not supported. There are two main clusters at the poles of a spectrum, but variability in the composition of gonads, genital shape and size, chromosomes and hormonal physiology. Rather than a discrete, 50:50 split there are many points of overlap between the designations of male and female.

Just as in physics with the contention that 'nature abhors a vacuum', so nature doesn't deal in dichotomies either.[22] This is the platform on which we need to consider gender.

THE GENDER PATH

Our assigned gender is founded on biological 'headlines' rather than the 'small print', that is, on the visual inspection of our anatomy using the more visible penis as its principle criterion. Its presence means 'It's a boy'; its absence means 'It's a girl'. The process continues along these lines:

biological sex	→	assigned gender	→	gender role	→	gender identity	→	gender expression
(penis/vagina)		(boy/girl)		(masculine/ feminine)		(internalization)		(externalization)

Whereas biological sex occurs irrespective of culture, our assigned gender is a social interpretation that triggers an elaborate system of cues that set up lifelong chains of expectation – rooted in the concepts of masculinity or femininity – of what it means to be a boy or a girl, a man or a woman. *Gender roles* (sometimes called *sex roles*) describe and prescribe distinct patterns of behaviour, providing a framework for how we interrelate with others, how we should fit in, how we dress, our mannerisms, our voices, as well as our sexual encounters, prospective partners, economic prosperity and even our personality. Gender roles may differ between different cultures at any given point in time. They may also change over time within the same culture.

Gender-role identity (or just *gender identity*) refers to the internalization of gender-role expectations, and what it means to identify as a girl or a boy, a woman or a man. It involves understanding and accepting that males and females are expected to be different from each other and to behave in contrary ways. Children become aware of their own gender identity around two and a half to three years of age, but possibly as early as 18 months. However, they still may entertain the idea that it is possible to crossover and change their gender.

A continuous and persistent sense of being one gender or 'the' other is known as *gender constancy*.[23] It's about grasping and accepting the idea that girls eventually become women and boys become men. It had been held that it was not until around ages six to seven that children grasp fully the idea that gender is a constant; that is, girls become women and boys become men. However, more recent research suggests that gender constancy may occur earlier, for some perhaps even as early as three years of age if children become aware of genital differences.[24] Gender constancy is made up of two factors: stability and consistency. Gender stability is a child's realization that boys grow up to be men and girls grow up to be women. Gender consistency refers to the knowledge that gender stays the same regardless of changes in the person's activities or appearance, such as behaving in a 'cross-gender' way.

Gender expression refers to its outward manifestation – its externalization. It is how individuals represent or express their gender identity to others, often through behaviour, clothing, hairstyles, voice or body characteristics. There is not necessarily a match between the gender we are assigned, how we internalize it and how we express it.

Not included in the chain of sex/gender development shown at the beginning of this section is *gender attribution*, which is the gender that others ascribe to us, depending on their perception of how we present ourselves. This is always based on partial information.

HOW WE ACQUIRE GENDER IDENTITY

Traditionally, there are three main psychological explanations of how we navigate the path to gender identity. These are *psychodynamic theory*, *social learning theory*, and *cognitive-developmental theory*. All focus on early childhood, that is, up until about seven years of age.[25]

Psychodynamic theory

Psychodynamic theories, following on from Sigmund Freud's psychoanalytic theory, focus on unconscious drives, the relationship of the child and early experiences with the parents (or primary caregivers). Gender is a core part of personality that rests on the child's awareness of its anatomy and its identification with the same-sex parent. The key point in its development is the resolution of the *Oedipus complex* for boys and the *Electra complex* for girls.[26] Both involve resolving an incestuous desire for the opposite-sex parent and competition with the same-sex parent. Girls view the same-sex parent as responsible for their loss of a penis. Boys fear that their penis will be taken away by the same-sex parent. This antagonism is somehow resolved, and the child aligns with the same-sex parent. For males, fear of the loss of the penis is a more abstract concept, meaning males must work harder to deal with uncertainty. For females, the loss is already apparent. On this view, the male role is stronger than is the female. It is not difficult to see the three gender lenses at work here.

Social learning theory

Instead of an innate, unconscious and biological basis of gender identity, *social learning theory*[27] emphasizes the child's environment and learning experiences. According to this view, gender roles are learned through a mixture of observing the behaviour of others and modelling (imitation of same-sex caregivers). Children recognize the differential behaviours of boys and girls, generally, and the treatment by others in the form of rewards or punishments for appropriate/inappropriate actions. Children also experience individual differences in treatment, which starts at birth with physical handling, clothes and toy choices and patterns of speech. Gender-linked behaviours are observable by age one. Through conditioning, behaviours regularly and consistently rewarded are most likely to persist, whereas those behaviours that are punished are more apt to cease.

Although *social learning theory* offers some explanation of how modelling and reinforcement interact, it tends to underplay individual differences in development and reactions from others such as inconsistencies in behavioural reinforcement. While it considers cognitive factors, it also underplays the agency of children and how they actively make sense of the world. It is also not clear how children cope with conflicting messages regarding gender.

Cognitive-developmental theory

According to the *cognitive-developmental theory*,[28] as children we mature and experience the world, reorganizing mental processes as we progress through a series of stages of development. Children's development hits various milestones moving from the simple to the complex and from the concrete to the abstract, including language development. Children are active agents in acquiring gender roles within development stages that allow for an increasingly sophisticated grasp of concepts and language. As children mature, discrepancies between their knowledge and their experiences of the environment cause their ideas to shift accordingly. The acquisition of gender constancy, stability and consistency can only happen when a child has reached a certain level of cognitive maturity.[29] According to this view, gender identity exists at several levels, possibly developing in line with language. A strong theme that emerges from the literature is that boys, more so than girls, value their own gender more highly.[30] This offers some support for the psychodynamic view that boys must try harder.

Overall, the psychology of gender is revealed in the grey areas, that is, the relationship between identity and expression, and how we make sense of the gaps between (biological) sex, self and the social. For many the mismatch gaps might be narrow or even imperceptible, others might find ways of behaving and thinking to bridge the divide, and yet for others, the divide can seem insurmountable.

TRANSGENDER, IPSO-GENDER, AGENDER, GENDERQUEER ETC. VERSUS CISGENDER

Whether arising from grass-roots activism or academic theory, the ever-expanding lexicon of gender identity terminology can be bewildering. In 2014, after a consultation exercise with LGBT advocacy organizations, social networking behemoth Facebook widened the debate by introducing a custom gender option with 50 terms for US users and later a further 21 for its UK audience. As well as female male, new options included variations of *trans*, *transgender* and *transsexual* as adjectives for a woman, a man and a person. A set of non-trans counterparts used the word *cisgender* or *cis*. There were also various labels including the word 'gender' such as *gender-fluid*, *gender-nonconforming*, *gender-variant*, *gender-neutral* and *genderqueer*. Others included *non-binary*, *polygender* and *agender*, as well as *intersex* and *two-spirit*. In 2015, Facebook expanded its system to offer a free-form field (for those using English), meaning unlimited scope for gender expression.[31] However, three years after the initial introduction, users only get two boxes to tick for who they are interested in: female or male!

Let's clarify the unfamiliar (and familiar) terminology in the gender compendium.

Transgender and transsexual

Transgender is perhaps the most recognized term to describe people whose gender identity (or expression) is different from that typically associated with their biological sex and assigned gender. It is correctly used as an adjective, not a noun ('transgender people' not 'transgenders').[32] The abbreviation trans is frequently used, sometimes with an asterisk (trans*) as an umbrella term that includes (but is not limited to) transgender, transsexual and cross-dressers (formerly described as transvestites). The asterisk has been the subject of fierce debate.[33] One view is that it was intended as a sign of inclusiveness for other non-binary genders, gender-questioning and gender-nonconforming identities, including genderqueer. However, in recent years, as LGBT has extended to LGBTQQIAPP+ suggesting the 'inclusive asterisk' has become redundant.[34] There is not universal agreement for how many items should be in the sequence to create a 'good enough' picture. The politics of gender and sexuality has become something of a battleground of terminology (visibility). An umbrella term incorporating all identities and co-communities is yet to be found and, more importantly, agreed upon.

Transsexual, a medical term from the 1940s has been largely supplanted by the more inclusive transgender. Part of the dissatisfaction with the term transsexual is the possible confusion with sexual orientation (that is, comparable with heterosexual, homosexual and bisexual).[35] Nevertheless, some people still use the term transsexual. To clarify, although all transsexual people are transgender, not all transgender people are transsexual. According to Kate Bornstein the common perception of transgender (when people don't know much about the subject) is of 'binary-identified transgender women and men'.[36] Sociologist Raewyn Connell found that whereas transgender stories mostly emphasize the fluidity of gender, transsexual autobiographies mostly emphasize gender's stability.[37] However people who subscribe to a binary model of gender might still describe themselves as transgender. Often transgender people are described as *postoperative* or *preoperative* – another binary. Bornstein includes nonoperative, recognizing that some people live in a gender identity opposite to the birth-assigned sex/gender but who 'have little or no intention of having genital and/or top (upper body) surgery'.[38]

From a medical perspective, *gender dysphoria* replaced the diagnosis of *gender identity disorder*. It takes emphasis away from perceptions of the disordered individual, to the personal distress associated with coping with the 'strong desires to be treated as the other gender or to be rid of one's sex characteristics, or a strong conviction that one has feelings and reactions typical of the other gender'.[39] The phrase 'the other gender', not '*another* gender', suggests that 'diagnosis' operates in a binary gender system.

Cisgender (or non-trans)?

Until the late 1990s, there was no term complementary to transgender, the closest being gender-normative – hardly a neutral term. To counter this, the term *cisgender* emerged in academic circles and was adopted by Facebook's gender terminology review. Whereas trans means 'across, beyond, through, outside of or changing thoroughly', cis means 'on this side of'. So, cisgender means 'everything lines up', that is, biological sex, assigned gender, gender identity and gender expression. Social justice entertainer and educator Sam Killerman describes cisgender as 'a politically sensitive replacement for normal'.[40] *Cisgenderism* works as a companion term with *sexism* and *heterosexism* to articulate an overall ideology of how people are valued in the (binary) sex and gender system.

Not surprisingly, the term is not without its critics. Some have questioned if it's a concept that's 'had its day' even before it has made the transition from academic circles to everyday usage.[41] I am usually suspicious of binary classifications in psychology, and argue that they should, more accurately, be expressed as continua.[42] Women's and gender studies writer Mimi Marinucci argues that for some, it is as self-defeating and as dangerous as the old masculine–feminine binary. It appears to lump lesbian, gay and bisexual people in the same category as heterosexual people implying that there is no mismatch between LGB experience and sociocultural expectations of assigned gender, gender identity and gender expression.[43] It is also question-able whether cisgender should be applied automatically to all straight (heterosexual) people. Krista Scott-Dixon maintains that the term 'non-trans' is clearer to average people than cisgender and may help to normalize trans people.[44] It shifts the emphasis to trans in the 'binary opposition' offering a more transcentric philosophical viewpoint.[45] Trans intersex scholar Cary Gabriel Costello argues that the trans–cis binary disregards the lives and experiences of people with intersex conditions, some of whom have been subjected to genital surgery. To counter this issue, Costello proposes the term *ipso-gender* (ipso mean-ing 'in the same place') for people with an intersex condition who identify with the sex they were assigned (by others) at birth.[46]

The Trans Student Educational Resources website defines cisgen-der as 'someone who exclusively identifies as their sex assigned at birth'. This would seem to limit, somewhat, the potential pool of candidates.[47] In personal declarations of gender, according to Killer-man, opting for cis-female or cis-male over 'plain old' female or male suggests the person has checked out all options and chosen the more emphatic cis.[48] It is not necessarily possible to tell whether a person identifies as 'ipso', 'trans' or 'cis' just by looking, so it is probably best not to presume.

So, what about other labels that flout the binary view?

Genderqueer and other non-binary terms

The lexical landscape is changing rapidly and many people are rejecting 'off-the-peg' gender labels in favour of something that resonates person-ally. So, what are the broad themes? Sam Killerman suggests, sardonically, that there is a sliding scale with gender-questioning and gender-non-conforming as 'entry level' labels with the more hard-core, 'in-your-face' genderqueer at the opposite end.[49] Gender-questioning does not (nec-essarily) reject the binary gender model, whereas genderqueer most emphatically does. Non-binary is often used as a general, collective term for gender positions resistant to the traditional binary view, as is gender-nonconforming. Both, to a certain degree, are defined by the thing they oppose. By contrast, genderqueer makes rebellion the default, and so offers a new paradigm for gender. It is sometimes used as an umbrella term for non-binary genders, but the use of 'queer' is considered too offensive for some.

Binary Gender   Gender-Questioning   Genderqueer

←——————————————————————————————————————→

Gender-fluid emphasizes adaptability, describing a person who 'goes with the flow' in that their gender may vary over time and according to circumstances, sometimes identifying as one of the binary options, another non-binary identity, or a combination. *Polygender* and *multi-gender* similarly affirm that gender is a 'many splendored thing'.

Agender, literally 'without gender', can mean someone does not identify with a specific gender or else do not consider gender to be of central importance in their lives (although it does not necessarily mean asexual). *Neutrois* is a catch-all 'gender neutral' label that can mean different things to different people, such as agender, neither/nor, genderless and so on. Androgyne (made up of 'andro' for man and 'gyne' for woman) is used by people who consider themselves to be both masculine and feminine, psychologically. All of this only scratches the surface. If in doubt, as with any gender label, ask people what it means to them.

With any gender label, there is a gap (or tension) between personal authenticity and social conformity and between self-identification and external imposition. The same is true of sexuality, and without consideration of this, our view of the gender landscape would not be complete.

SEXUALITY, HAVING SEX AND SEX/GENDER ROLES

Numerous writers make the link between how we have sex (sexuality) and gender identity. Cultural anthropologist Gayle Rubin categorizes sex as a *Charmed Circle* versus the *Outer Limits*, that is, in which it is considered 'good, normal, natural and blessed' versus 'bad, the abnormal, the unnatural, and the damned'.[50] Rubin contends that sex is validated according to series of interconnecting binaries, including whether it is heterosexual or homosexual, procreative versus recreational, married versus unmarried, monogamous versus polyamorous (promiscuous) and so on. Sexuality in the Charmed Circle begins with one man and one woman. From the platform of binary gender, the default option for sexuality is heterosexuality, that is, sexual attraction and behaviour between adults of the 'opposite sex'. Hetero is taken to mean 'different', and this implies a difference or complementarity in genitals, that is, in the most basic of terms, 'vagina/penis' sex. Heterosexuality is based on what Judith Butler describes as 'the production of discrete and asymmetrical oppositions between "feminine" and "masculine"'.[51] The hetero/homo distinction also represents a gender 'deviation' (but more so for men). According to Michael Warner in The Trouble with Normal, heterosexuality is more than just sexual behaviour and attraction between adults with different genitals. It is the name for a whole package of assumptions that aim to reduce the enormous variety of human capacity and experience into a predictable consensus of outcomes.[52] One of these assumptions, reduces lesbian sex to heterosexual foreplay.[53] According to Kate Bornstein, masculinity and heterosexuality are the principle factors in defining 'perfect gender'.[54]

In a series of experiments (including attitudes to the body, as mentioned earlier) I found support for these theoretical insights. The results demonstrated that heterosexual men were rated more masculine, and heterosexual women were rated more feminine, than their gay/lesbian counterparts. In a further analysis, gay men and lesbian women were rated more highly on a measure of gender nonconformity than their straight counterparts. Differences were even more marked for the sample of male participants. Overall, the results indicated that homophobia is in part a function of attitudes to gender-role non-conformity and is related to sexism.

Challenging the binary view, in the 1940s and 1950s Alfred Kinsey and colleagues proposed a model of sexuality expressed as a continuum. Although academic books, Kinsey's two volumes on sexual behaviour became mainstream best sellers and caused a public sensation at the time. Instead of a 'binary-genital-preference' model, Kinsey offered two seven-point scales, one to express sexual behaviour and one for sexual attraction:

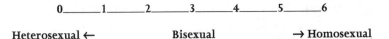

A Kinsey zero represents no same-sex behaviour or attraction, and a Kinsey six represents only same-sex behaviour and attraction. Notably, there are five shades of bisexuality in between (one to five on the scale). Separating attraction and behaviour render absolute 'all-or-nothing' sexual identities less inevitable. More recent research supports the view that although related, behaviour and attraction are not perfectly correlated. Looking at three national samples (USA, UK and France) one study found whereas between 2.1% and 3.6% of females reported having some same-sex experience, between 17.8% and 18.5% reported experiencing same-sex behaviour or attraction. For males, between 4.5% and 10.7% of males had experienced some form of same-sex behaviour, and between 16.3% and 20.8% had experienced same-sex behaviour or attraction.[55] Arguably, sexual attraction has more to do with gender expression whereas sexual behaviour is just genital expression. Feasibly, we might be attracted to someone *despite* genitalia, not because of it. In Kinsey's scheme, bisexuality is more intelligible rather than disparaged as transient, confused or greedy, from the binary view.

Although Kinsey's insights made the leap from academia to popular imagination, today, the Kinsey continuum still mainly finds currency in academic circles. In everyday life and the pop-psychology imagination, the binary model continues to dominate.

CONCLUSIONS

In this chapter, we have considered the relationship between sex and gender, particularly the notion that gender is predicated on an incontestable line between the sexes. We have examined biological sex and found that it is not an accurate picture of what happens in reality. At the level of chromosomes, hormones and genitals, nature does not deal in absolutes. There are multiple points of variation from the binary theme and areas of overlap rather than discrete categories. Rather than hard-and-fast constructs, we have 'fuzzy approximations' and areas of ambiguity. Based on a less secure footing, gender is also subject to multiple points of variation and interpretation. The explosion of self-identifying labels suggests that gender is shifting from a social identity to a social *and* personal one.

Chapter 3 considers, in greater depth, the mechanisms by which we make sense of sex, gender and life as a whole, and specifically examines psychological explanations for why we are drawn to binary classifications. We examine a fourth model of development (schema theory) closely aligned with the development of gender stereotypes. The chapter also deals with the hidden assumptions associated with such stereotypes and tests their validity by examining sex (gender) differences, both physical and psychological, in research.

3

GENDER STEREOTYPES AND SEX DIFFERENCES

The premise of 'biological inevitability' lends a sense of authenticity, naturalness or 'realness' to patterns of gender. We might even regard some people as 'all man' or 'all woman'. Such idealized portraits are known as *gender-role stereotypes* – seemingly descriptive but often prescriptive. These ideals form the basis of many a best-selling, pop-psychology book on relationships. This chapter considers some of the psychological mechanisms (schema theory and attitudes) we employ to create and maintain gender-role stereotypes. These help to explain why black-and-white categories are so compelling. It goes on to examine research findings on psychological gender differences to ascertain whether we are worlds apart or all on the same page. Finally, the chapter sets the scene for discussing alternatives to the binary gender approach (later in the book) by considering the concept of androgyny.

MAKING SENSE OF THE WORLD

Two overlapping psychological concepts help to understand how we organize our knowledge of ourselves, others and the world: *schemata* and *attitudes*. They can be thought of as a form of human computer software – key procedures in our brain's operating system.

Schema theory

In a rapidly changing environment, it is impossible to process afresh every particle of information that impinges upon us every waking minute of every day. Our brains (and our heads) would need to be huge to accommodate the increased cognitive load. So how do our brains cope?

We have a need to create an orderly world with governable rules. To achieve this, our pattern-seeking brain employs various routines and 'rule-of-thumb' (heuristic) shortcuts. Many situations, especially familiar ones, do not need sophisticated analysis, just automatic responses. A *schema* (plural *schemata*, sometimes schemas) is a mental structure of preconceived ideas representing some aspect of the world – a kind of 'brain app'. As children, we actively construct a series of schemata based on social interactions, experiences and observations. These provide frameworks to organize existing knowledge and shape new experience. They focus our attention, filter our perceptions, shape memories and plug the gaps in our knowledge with their most-likely-default values. Schemata help us to forecast and predict likely events, assess threats, make decisions and regulate behaviour.[1] We develop schemata about categories of information, specific situations or events (such as going out to a restaurant), how things work (e.g. cars, computers, etc.), in fact about almost everything including ourselves, other people and social roles (including gender).

Social psychologist Sandra Bem contends that information about gender is passed on and maintained within society through schemata starting in childhood. *Gender Schema Theory* is based on elements of social learning and cognitive developmental theories (from Chapter 2). Gender schemata include cultural blueprints of maleness and femaleness, how we and others fit in and how to recognize 'real' men and 'real' women. Schemata do more than just influence day-to-day experiences; they also shape our whole world view and life choices. However, the processing advantages come at a cost, and maintaining our schemata is a balancing act. When new information conflicts with our schemata it produces an unpleasant state of disequilibrium[2] (a state of flux or uncertainty), which we are motivated to reduce. Schemata might heighten some stimuli and downplay others, more often focusing on stuff that fits. This makes them resistant to change, even in the face of conflicting evidence. Often, their 'best-guess, default-values' override, re-interpret or distort new information. For example, research has shown that children whose gender schemata are well-developed tend to remember pictures of men and women acting in traditional gender stereotyped ways better than counter-stereotypical images. Recall of images is also distorted to fit the stereotype; for example, seeing a picture of a man ironing is remembered as a woman ironing.[3]

It is common to ask the gender of a baby before interacting with it, if there are no obvious signs. Simple colour coding (pink or blue) is enough to trigger our 'delicate little girl' or 'big strong boy' schemata. In a psychology experiment, adults were asked to rate the emotional behaviour of nine-month-old infants. Observing the child with a 'jack in the box', the adults reported different emotions depending on the perception of gender (fear for girls and anger for boys). Other researchers found a similar pattern when observing adults interacting with 14-month-old children. When a child was introduced as a boy, the adults selected masculine toys and encouraged more physical activity. By contrast, when introduced as a girl, interactions with the child were more verbal and nurturing.[4] Same baby; different schemata.

Considering the related psychological topic of attitudes helps to explain individual differences in information processing.

The function of attitudes

Attitude literally means 'fit and ready for action'. Attitudes are the starting blocks, the 'on your marks and get ready' before you go. It's useful, for this discussion, to think of attitudes as the drivers for schemata (as there is a cross over between them). Psychologist Elliot Katz asserts that attitudes serve four primary functions, best considered as four aspects of an interactive process.[5] Consider each of these in the context of gender roles:

At the most basic level, attitudes fulfil an *instrumental function* in evaluating our likes and dislikes and broadly categorizing things as good/bad, positive/negative, appropriate/inappropriate, masculine/ feminine, useful/useless and so on. In this way, attitudes help us to maximize gains and minimize losses as we are drawn to things that benefit us and repelled by things that disadvantage us. Second, attitudes serve a *knowledge function* by helping us to organize and structure information and perceptions about the world. Our attitudes change when faced with overwhelming contradictory evidence and so we alter our frame of reference (schemata). Third, they provide a *value-expression function*, that is, to reinforce our self-image, our sense of who we are (including our gender identity) and the values we represent. Their fourth function is *ego-defensiveness*. That is, they help us maintain our sense of self, and protect us from uncomfortable home-truths and the harsher realities of life, such as not living up to gender ideals.

Schemata and attitudes are implicated in stereotyping, which we consider later. Before that, we consider binary thinking, a key theme rippling through all discussions of gender and sexuality (This sentence seems to have triggered my ice cream schemata.).

BINARY THINKING

As the saying goes, 'there are two types of people in this world: those who believe the world can be split into binary categories and those who don't'. Binary thinking is key to organizing thoughts and concepts. It is the default processing option when we are subject to stress. We do not have time to process the nuances we need quickly to handle threat or non-threat, fight or flight.[6] At a cultural level, we use philosophical laws that act as a meta-program for organizing knowledge.[7]

Laws of (Western) thought

When classifying gender and sexuality, or any situation where we define an identity, such as sports teams, three laws of thought come into play:

1 *The law of identity*, which states: Whatever is, is.
2 *The law of contradiction*, which states: Nothing can both be and not be.
3 *The law of excluded middle*, which states: Everything must either be or not be.

In short, we create labels, define their qualities and behaviours and exclude anything that is ambiguous or does not fit.[8] With colonialism and imperialism, these laws extended across much of the globe, as has the binary gender model.[9] The gender lenses of biological essentialism and gender polarity operate in accord with these laws. In discussions of sex and gender, the law of excluded middle is critical. LGBTQI+: (sometimes written as 'LGBTIQ+') people occupy these grey areas. Examining these laws and lenses makes negative attitudes to 'otherness' more intelligible. Biphobia has been described as 'the fear of space between our categories'.[10]

Intolerance of ambiguity and personal need for structure

After the Second World War, the need to understand how fascism could have taken hold with such disastrous consequences motivated Theodore Adorno and colleagues to research the *Authoritarian Personality*. This research yielded various psychometric measures including *intolerance of ambiguity* (IA). High scores on IA indicate people with a stronger preference for black and white categories. High intolerance of ambiguity is related to negative attitudes to gender non-conformity, and negative attitudes to homosexuality. A similar concept, *personal need for structure* (PNS), also measures the need for cognitive and behavioural simplicity. High PNS scores are significant predictors of negative attitudes towards lesbians and gay men. From a purely cognitive perspective, for people with a strong personal need for structure, LGBTQI+ people just 'overcomplicate things'.[11]

Social psychologist, Gordon Allport argues that prejudice (literally 'to pre-judge') represents, in part, a greater cognitive need use 'either/or' dichotomies (binaries). Sticking to tried and tested habits and, where possible, embracing the familiar, simple and definite (and hence safe) all meet this need. Allport contends that prejudiced children are more likely (than their non-prejudiced counterparts) to hold the view that people can be divided into two types: 'the weak and the strong'. Adults show similar tendencies, where racially prejudiced males hold that there are only two kinds of women: 'the pure and the bad'.[12]

All the preceding provides a platform on which to examine gender-role stereotypes.

STEREOTYPES, POP-PSYCHOLOGY AND GENDER

Stereotypes are packets of knowledge that contain schematized sets of attitudes, beliefs and (over-) generalizations about the characteristics, psychological traits and behaviours of a group or class of individuals. For gender, they incorporate ideas of what it means to be a 'real' man and 'real' woman. When applied to people, they provide quick thumbnail sketches to help simplify the social world and predict certain behaviours. Generally, stereotypes have negative connotations, and the main downside is that they set up a tendency to 'pigeon-hole' people, meaning we interact with the stereotype rather than the person before us.[13] Stereotypes also foster a tribal 'us and them' mentality in the social world. Research shows that it takes surprisingly little for us to form a commitment to a group. In one experiment children were assigned to a red group or a blue group (with T-shirts). Researchers found that even allocation to a control condition (with no reinforcement of the merits of group membership) was enough to bias children's choice of toys and playmates.[14] A group based on anatomical difference – with a lifetime of reinforcement – is even more likely to forge a sense of in-group allegiance.

In pop-psychology talk, we hear of men 'getting in touch with their feminine sides', implying emotions, traits and skills can be divided, neatly, into clusters of maleness and femaleness. Male character traits circle around the master trait of competency. For females, the central trait is nurturance.[15] This tendency is not specific to gender. It is a recognized phenomenon in social psychology known as the halo effect. It's part of our 'infer-a-personality' schema. With one trait, we 'best-guess' a fuller psychological profile. In a classic experiment (by social psychologist Solomon Asch) two groups of participants were given a list of traits describing a fictitious person. The lists only varied on one trait – one group had 'warm' and the other 'cold'. When asked to indicate, from a second list, which words best described the person, the 'warm trait' group chose generous, humorous, sociable and popular whereas the 'cold trait' group chose the opposites.[16]

Pop-psychology books closely adhere to gender-role stereotypes, which explains their appeal, as they 'entertain' with humorous and reassuring familiarity. Stereotypes (like schemata) have their own 'self-fulfilling' filtering system. This means they contain a 'mixed-bag' of information from facts, half-truths, common-knowledge, myths, gossip, propaganda, and tabloid sensationalism. Research findings, when incorporated – for stereotypes and pop-psychology books – are usually self-serving. They are invariably used selectively or uncritically, or are often out-of-date.[17] For instance, pop-psychology's 'right-brain/left-brain' distinction is based on research from 1968 (and the early 1970s). Clearly, neuroscience has not stood still for half a century. First the simplistic 'two-brain' terminology is misleading. We have one brain with two hemispheres with some specialization but with extensive interaction. More recent research using Magnetic Resonance Imaging (MRI) did not find evidence of hard-and-fast, lateralized brain types.[18] However, this does not offer attention-grabbing headlines. The same applies to research on gender. In popular media, cutting-edge theory and research is overlooked in favour of the stereotypical and 'easily digestible'. Evidence-based research challenging the 'battle of the sexes' is often derided and dismissed as 'political correctness gone mad'.

Academia is not immune to the lure of the stereotype. In the previous chapter, we saw how gender lenses distort our view of the human body. In *The Egg and the Sperm*, Emily Martin maintains that science has 'constructed a romance' based on gender-role stereotypes to explain the reproductive process.[19] Accounts often convey the impression that female biological processes are 'less worthy' than male counterparts. Egg production is often described as 'wasteful', but sperm over-production is often overlooked. Male processes are described as active, agentic, strong and efficient. By contrast, the egg is shed or disposed of or is passively swept along. According to Martin, it was not until the mid-1980s that biologists revised the view of the sperm as the forceful penetrator, finding its thrust is relatively weak, and its strongest tendency is to pry itself off the egg. Nevertheless, sperm were still described as attacking and penetrating, only a little less forcefully. Only in the late 1980s was the egg credited with a more active role and instead cast as an aggressive sperm catcher to compensate for the insufficient thrust from the sperm.[20] Although, the egg and sperm are partners, the process is more akin to building bridges than to fighting battles, the model of domination and submission prevails in the popular imagination. By viewing the sperm and the egg through gender lenses they are endowed with non-existent (unequal) social identities.

In the next section, we consider the defining qualities of gender stereotypes and the implications.

THE GOLD STANDARD: REAL WOMEN AND REAL MEN

What does it mean to be a 'real man' or a 'real woman'? Is there a gold standard from a golden age? Here we consider two gender blueprints, one each for femininity and masculinity. Both emphasize conforming to external yardsticks and suppressing individual differences.

The cult of womanhood

In the 1960s, Barbara Welter coined the term 'the cult of womanhood'.[21] Based on an analysis of the new role created for upper and middle-class white women during the mid-19th century, these historical snapshots still inform pop-psychology books today. Welter offers four cardinal virtues – piety, purity, submissiveness and domesticity. The overarching themes are women should be cooperative, inward-looking, relationship-oriented. All cultivate feelings of guilt.

Piety in a non-religious sense means that women are seen as more dutiful and held to a higher moral standard than are men. Consequently, there is harsher judgement for a woman who leaves her children than there is for a man. Colloquially, mothers are described as 'saints', putting the needs of others before their own.

Purity in the sexual sense means that the promiscuous woman is the subject of more scorn than is the promiscuous man (the double standard of the red-blooded male versus the 'not very nice girl'). There are also greater pressures on women (notably from magazines) with never-ending prescriptions to maintain the purity of the temple of the body.

The virtue of submissiveness means deference to the authority of men. Whereas assertive men are 'go-getters', assertive women are described as 'man-haters' or 'total bitches' (or worse) and accused of emasculating men. Fitting in with a male-centred world, it's held that women's goals are better achieved through 'feminine wiles' and massaging the egos of men. Certain words are (gender) schemata in themselves. Consider the definition of 'vagina', literally a sheath for a sword. It suggests that a woman's sexual role is defined in terms of the (passive and utilitarian) function it serves for men. A rather unsettling example of this can be seen in one of John Gray's *Mars and Venus in the Bedroom*, which has the sole purpose of creating the right conditions to ensure coitus for men to be 'teleported out of the dry domain of his intellectual detachment into the moist caverns of sensitive and sensuous feeling'.[22] According to cultural studies scholar Annie Potts the guilt-trip for woman is 'denial of sex for men . . . becomes tantamount to denial of existence for men'.[23] In *The Female Eunuch* feminist and scholar Germaine Greer argues that women are forced to assume submissive roles in society to fulfil male fantasies of what being a woman entails.[24] In short, in stereotypical terms, *men wield; women yield.*

Domesticity and femininity are inextricably linked in the domestic goddess archetype. Women are still responsible for most of the household duties in a male–female relationship, even when both are in full-time employment.[25] Even in same-sex relationships based on a heterosexual model, the (supposedly) more feminine of the partners takes care of the domestic duties.[26]

The cult of womanhood is also about the personal; in contrast, the male gender stereotype is all about the positional.

The cardinal pillars of manhood

In the 1970s, Richard Brannon proposed the four cardinal aspirations of masculinity, which have been less resistant to change than the virtues of womanhood. They are:

1 No Sissy Stuff – the need to be different to females.
2 The Big Wheel – the need to be superior to others.
3 The Sturdy Oak – the need to be self-reliant and independent.
4 Give 'em Hell – the need to be more powerful than others.

The theme of 'no sissy stuff' (sometimes 'no girly stuff') is more than anti-femininity; accurately, it is anti-effeminacy, emphasizing the links between misogyny and homophobia. Homophobia is not just same-sex-behaviour prejudice; it also serves to police masculinity generally. Real men should be free (unambiguously) from any sign of 'the other'. Effeminacy is bad, quite literally. The word comes from 'baedling' which meaning 'womanish man'. So, whereas 'real men' might be amenable, occasionally, to getting in touch with their feminine sides, they are unlikely to boast of getting in touch with their gay sides. Also, consider the supposedly neutral word 'homosexual' – coined in the age of the steam engine – originally a medical diagnosis for a form of impotence (literally 'loss of power') which left the sufferer with a fear of the opposite sex. Consequently, homosexual men were deemed unable to resist the domination of real men.[27] It was not until the second decade of the 20th century that 'homosexual' came to refer to both partners.[28] The passive role in sex is a loss of position literally and figuratively. Power and status are integral to idealized male sexual performance (and position in society).

Some implicit assumptions in the development of psychometric tests also reflect gender hierarchy. In the 1930s, the *Attitude Interest Analysis Survey* consisted of 456 items to measure masculinity and femininity. Items typically endorsed by males were termed M items, and those usually endorsed by females were called F items. The final score comes from subtracting the total F score from the M score giving a positive result for masculinity and negative for femininity. However, the method for devising the Mf (uppercase M, lower case f) subscale of the Minnesota Multiphasic Personality Inventory (MMPI) (first published in the 1940s) is bizarre. Only men were used to validate the Mf scale. For the masculine items, they used heterosexual (or at least not 'out') soldiers. However, for the validation of the feminine scale, they didn't bother to include women in the sample but instead used 13 (known) 'homosexual' men.[29] The MMPI is a leading personality test still in use today (although hopefully there have been some methodological refinements).

For masculinity, the 'big wheel' represents status, success and respect. Set in competition with others it is all about being number one, the 'top-dog', the alpha male archetype. In Zero and One, performance artist Laurie Anderson proclaims, 'Everybody wants to be number one, and no one wants to be a nothing'.[30] In the traditional 'missionary position' in sex, men are on top. In the gay sexual jargon, the penetrative partner is called 'the top', and the penetrated partner is the bottom. In China, gay men's roles in sex are characterized by zeroes and ones – as rudimentary symbols for anatomy (anus = 0, penis = 1). The 'one', the top, has higher status than the 'zero' (the bottom).[31] However, this distinction has become blurred with the advent of the 'power bottom'. This is someone in a receptive role with 'a lot of endurance' or someone, although in the receptive role, that takes a more dominant role in sex, also called a 'dominant bottom'. The distinction has also been blurred on heterosexual encounters in the sex act known as pegging. Here the woman takes the penetrative role (with a sex aid) in anal sex with a man.

In an experiment to examine attitudes to roles in non-procreative (that is, recreational) sex acts, participants were presented with four scenarios and asked which partner was most likely to initiate the act:

1 Male penis penetrating female anus (standard heterosexual).
2 Female with penis-shaped object penetrating male anus (reversed heterosexual – pegging).
3 Male penis penetrating male anus (gay male).
4 Female with penis-shaped object penetrating female anus (lesbian).

In the standard heterosexual couple, the male actor was most often identified as the initiator (in keeping with stereotypes). For the gay couple, the penetrator (the top) was indicated as more likely to initiate – confirming the association between the active penetrator and the passive receiver. However, in the reversed heterosexual scenario, the (penetrated) male was still judged more likely to have initiated the act. The person with the real 'inactive' penis took precedence over the one with the substitute 'active' one. In short, men are judged to be dominant/power bottoms in these encounters. When asked about instigation for lesbian and gay couples, there were less marked differences in which role was instigator; in short, it was more of a mutual decision. The most frequently cited reason for instigation in the heterosexual couples (standard and reversed) was 'receiving pleasure' for the male. When the male was in the receptive ('passive') role with a female, the second most frequently cited reason was (his) 'personal choice'. 'Power' was associated with the active (penetrator) role. For some presumably in the reversed heterosexual couple, the male exercised 'personal choice' to give up 'power' in exchange for 'receiving pleasure'.[32]

Common to all four themes of 'true manhood' is the self-evaluation by external benchmarks. Much of the male role is predicated on bluster and bravado, what George Weinberg (the psychologist who coined 'homophobia') calls the 'masculine pretence'[33] – extremely compliant at being fiercely independent, socially expansive but emotionally bottled-up 'Real men' are not true to themselves. Little boys quickly learn that big boys don't cry. Many of the characteristics associated with masculinity, such as aggressiveness, ambition, success, striving virility, competitiveness, are intrinsically tied to the pressure and expectation that 'real' men should maintain dominion over others. Compared with the female gender role, the male role has been less amenable to change over the years.[34] Existential philosopher and feminist scholar Simone de Beauvoir, in *The Second Sex*, argues that man is considered the default, while woman is considered the 'other'.[35] This informs Kate Bornstein's claim that in the binary system perfect gender is male.[36]

The idea that there are some people who exemplify the 'real deal', suggests that not all of us 'make the grade'. This implies spectrum of gender, rather than all-or-nothing.

Gender stereotypes, personality clusters and genital morphology

From the stereotyped view of gender, the psychological world is divided into two groups: the masculine and the feminine. Members of each group share skill sets, interests and personality traits, which are different and distinct from the other group.[37] For a graphical representation, see Figure 3.1.

The masculine group inhabited by males is outer-directed with a master trait of competency or agency. Its halo of corresponding traits includes being assertive (aggressive), adventurous, forceful and achievement oriented. By contrast, the feminine group inhabited by females is inner-directed with a 'master' trait of nurturance or expressiveness. Its halo of corresponding traits includes being communal, selfless, sentimental, submissive and other-centred. However, nothing in psychology neatly divides into all-or-nothing categories. In psychometric tests (including personality tests), the cardinal rule is that a trait cannot be measured accurately using a single item. It is okay for magazine tests, but does not pass muster in scientific tests.

An observation from psychologist Erik Erickson reveals the lens of biological essentialism in corroborating gender-role stereotypes.

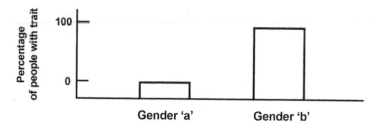

Figure 3.1 The binary view of gender difference for any given trait

Describing children at play he concluded that boys create tall towers and structures whereas girls create more internal, domestic-type scenes. In other words, reasoning that children perhaps unconsciously recreate the respective shapes of their genitals in play scenarios. Psychotherapist Eric Berne describes the male genitals as 'an aggressive delivery system', contrasting with female genitals as being 'equipped to encourage and handle . . . deliveries'. Instead of using 'women' and 'men', human rights author and gender theorist Martine Rothblatt in The Apartheid of Sex refers to women as 'people with vaginas' and men as 'people with penises'.[38] Gender stereotypes are nothing more than genital metaphors – males (the number ones) have 'outy' personalities and females (the zeroes) have 'innies'. Despite our evolutionary and cultural advances, from a binary model of gender we are still expected to live up (or down) to our genitals.

Next, we consider evidence from research on gender differences to assess the validity of gender polarity.

HOW DIFFERENT ARE WE REALLY?

Before considering gender differences in research, it is important to clarify what we mean by research.

What is research?

Used in an informal sense, research might mean a trawl of the Internet, canvassing the opinions of friends or the inclusion of a few percentages to bolster an advertising campaign. Academic research strives to be more rigorous, designed according to scientific principles and ethical guidelines and with a more cautious interpretation of its findings. Academic research undergoes a peer-review process, that is, it is scrutinized by other academics before it is published.

Quantitative research has a two-stage process for the statistical analysis of data. First a descriptive stage using group averages (means, medians or modes), measures the spread of scores and percentages. The second stage involves tests to assess whether observed differences are *statistically significant*. We cannot claim a significant difference at the descriptive stage. We must test for it and be more than 95% confident that results did not occur due to chance or error, that is, odds of more than 19:1 against. However, we still need to distinguish between a difference that looks good on paper (one that only a statistician could get excited about) and *ecological validity*, that is, one that is likely to have real world significance.

Sex/gender differences in research

To consolidate the results (and balance out any errors) of many studies to arrive at an overall (hopefully[39] more robust) bottom line, statisticians use a technique called a *meta-analysis*. In meta-analyses, the effect size is expressed as a mean difference between the groups in a standard score (*d*, also known as Cohen's *d*).[40] In research on gender differences it allows us to assess not only the size of the differences between male and female groups but also the degree of overlap between groups. For ease of comparison, but with caution,[41] we can group the scores from meta-analyses into five broad categories based on the size of '*d*': *small, small to moderate, moderate, moderate to large and large*.[42] Again, positive values of *d* indicate male superiority and negative values indicate female superiority.

In 2005, in her paper *The Gender Similarities Hypothesis*, psychologist Janet Shibley Hyde remarked that the first major review of gender differences, in 1974, found more evidence for gender similarity, with just four areas of notable difference (verbal ability, visual-spatial ability, mathematical ability and aggression). Textbooks reporting the research focused almost exclusively on these differences. In her updated review, Hyde examined 46 meta-analyses from a 20-year period on gender differences. This yielded 124 effects sizes (*d* values). More than three-quarters (78%) were either *close to zero* or in the *small* range. The prominent differences were that compared with females, males could throw further and faster, were more physically aggressive, masturbated more and held attitudes that were more positive to sex in uncommitted relationships.[43] Some might argue that this just about sums up the 'typical bloke'.

Before looking at some of the main differences usually associated with gender,[44] statistician and psychologist Jacob Cohen – who laid the foundations for meta-analysis – offers a few familiar comparisons to help put figures into context. A *moderate* d value (0.50) represents the difference in height between 15 and 16-year-old females. This means your chance of guessing age from height would be about 60%. A *large* d value (1.00) is like the difference in height between 13 and 18-year-old females. Your chance of guessing age from height is now about 69%. The difference in height between males and females of the same age is around 2.00, that is, *very large*. This equates to an 84% chance of guessing gender from height.

Throwing things – as we would expect physical height and size differences translate into comparable differences in physical ability. On average, males can throw things further and at a greater velocity than can females. Both differences are *very large* (with d around +2.00).

Attitudes to sex – as there is a double standard in sexual activity between men and women, it's also not surprising that research shows large gender differences in sexual attitudes. For reported frequency of masturbation, the difference is *large* (d = +0.96). It is important to note that this is reported frequency; the true figures might be different. However, based on this statistic, you could correctly guess gender about 68% of the time. For attitudes to non-committed (casual) sex the difference is also *large* (d = +0.81) – a correct guess 66% of the time. For ratings of sexual satisfaction, the difference between males and females is close to zero (d = −0.06), which means almost total overlap.

Aggression – is one key area where research, to a certain degree, aligns with the stereotype of the aggressive male. However, it is not totally clear cut. The most reliable finding is for physical aggression with differences in the ranges from moderate (d = +0.40), moderate to large (d = +0.50 to 0.60) and large (d = +0.84). Taking the average (0.50) you would guess gender from scores 60% of the time. Relational aggression is a more complex type of aggression, often less observable, such as excluding others or damaging reputations through gossiping. For this type, females show higher scores (d up to −0.74, that is, in the moderate to large range) – you would guess gender correctly 65% of the time. However, for both direct and indirect aggression the results vary depending on context. It is not all about gender.

Verbal ability – is, according to the stereotype, where females excel. The research does indicate that females do perform better than males but not 'different planet' different – it is in the statistically *small* range ($d = -0.11$). To put it into context, of the people scoring above average on verbal ability tests, 53% would be female and 47% male. According to Hyde, another way of looking at this is that 99% of the difference in scores is due to something other than gender. The differences (female superiority) are more notable, that is, edging into the moderate range, for adolescents for spelling ($d = -0.45$), meaning a correct guess for gender 59% of the time.

Mathematical abilities – are where males are supposed to excel. However, research indicates that gender differences in mathematics are often a function of age and the type of mathematical ability tested. Taken across all groups and all types of mathematical performance, the male edge is in the small range ($d = +0.15$). The main gender difference emerges in adolescence with male superiority for problem solving. The difference is in the *small to moderate* range ($d = +0.30$). Overall, the findings indicate that the gap is narrowing. An interesting aspect is the difference between self-confidence and anxiety in relation to mathematical ability. Males are more likely to score higher on measures of confidence ($d = +0.16$) and females are more likely to score higher on measures of anxiety ($d = -0.15$).

Helpfulness – according to gender-role stereotypes being helpful is more pronounced in females – which is presumably why AI helper applications (such as Siri and Cortana) are feminized. However, research does not support this. Overall, men are more likely to engage in helping behaviour. However, this difference is only *small to moderate* ($d = +0.13$). Research shows that context is important. When there's no surveillance, the gender difference is *close to zero* ($d = -0.02$). When there is surveillance, the gender difference is *moderate to large* ($d = +0.74$), with men more likely to be helpful.

In their paper, *Men and Women Are from Earth: Examining the Latent Structure of Gender*, social psychologists Bobbi Carothers and Harry Reis[45] conclude that although there are average differences between men and women, these differences are more dimensional than categorical, and inappropriate for 'diagnosing' gender-typical psychological variables based on biological sex. To answer the question of how far categorical differences in genitals extend to other aspects of human biology, psychologist Daphna Joel and her colleagues analyzed MRI (Magnetic Resonance Imaging) scans of more than 1400 human brains. Acknowledging that although there are documented sex/gender differences in the brain, the notion of a sexually dimorphic view ('male brain' versus 'female brain') only makes sense if there is little overlap between the brain features and if they are internally consistent, that is, male-only versus female-only features. They found that brains with features consistently at one end of the 'maleness–femaleness' continuum are rare. Human brains do not belong to one of two distinct categories: male brain/female brain; rather, most brains are comprised of unique 'mosaics' of features.[46] Not known for 'pulling her punches', cognitive neuroscientist Gina Rippon, who describes the different planet approach as 'neurotrash', argues that Joel and colleagues' findings are 'a major challenge to the entrenched misconceptions typified by the "men are from Mars, women are from Venus" hokum'.[47] Neuroscientist and author Cordelia Fine (who coined the term 'neurosexism') makes the point that many of the arguments for 'hardwired' gender differences often overlook the fact that behaviour changes can lead to brain changes. So, although raised testosterone can lead to increased aggression, it is equally true that aggressive behaviour can raise testosterone. As she argues, 'one-way arrows of causality are just so last century'.[48]

Evolutionary psychologist Marco Del Giudice (and colleagues), however, challenges the methodology of Joel and colleagues claiming that some of their criteria are so strict that 'there seems to be no degree of sexual dimorphism in realistic datasets that will yield results that falsify the hypotheses of Joel et al'.[49] So even something, seemingly, as sure as a brain scan is subject to a 'Gun Fight at the Methodological Corral'. Del Giudice anticipates that 'combining multiple sources of brain imaging data (e.g., volume, thickness, connectivity) would make it possible to identify a person's gender from his/her brain structure with considerable accuracy'.[50] So, how do we make sense of bewildering conflicting evidence? The reverse of Del Giudice's statement must also be true. We might be able to identify a person's 'social interpretation of their biological sex' from scans of their brain structure. The conclusion? Gender can really mess with your head! It's facetious but equally valid.

In discussions of gender differences, both sides of the debate acknowledge there is a crossover. The dispute is about how much. So, rather than the two disconnected blocks as seen in Figure 3.1, it is more accurate to assign percentage figures and represent each gender as a bell-shaped curve (representing the normal distribution of scores). The majority of scores cluster around the middle, with decreasing frequencies approaching either of the tails, so there are few very low or very high scores. The overlap or crossover ('the grey area') represents the degree of similarity. The size of the crossover varies depending on the trait. In some cases, the similarity can be greater than the difference (see Figure 3.2). Obviously, zero difference equals total overlap.

This over-lapping curve arrangement is the same for the biological differences examined in Chapter 2. The curves might be steeper and the overlap might be smaller, but the principle is the same.

Overall, the case for the 'different-planet' view would be more compelling if most of the statistical differences were in the 2.00 to 3.00 range. Even then, there would still be crossover. The reality is

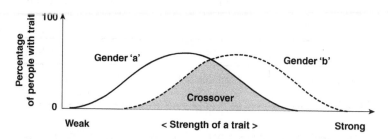

Figure 3.2 Overlapping curves of gender difference for any given trait

that many differences are around 0.20. From her review, Hyde concluded that from childhood to adulthood, overall, males and females are more alike than different on most psychological variables. It is, however, important to consider the impact of small differences in terms of academic achievement. How we interpret and act on the difference might be more important than the difference itself, again, the viewing influences the doing. A notable trend from meta-analyses on gender differences is that the gaps are narrowing over time, especially the small to moderate ones. Undoubtedly, social, political and economic changes regarding the rights, roles and expectations of men and women have helped to bring this about. Given the 'necessary and sufficient conditions'[51] for change – things change; people change.

ANDROGYNY

After reviewing various analytic studies, psychologist Anne Constantinople argues that measures of masculinity and femininity more likely tap into several independent, separate clusters of beliefs and attitudes. On this view, gender is multidimensional, not binary.[52] Also in the 1970s psychologist Sandra Bem changed perceptions about gender roles by putting masculinity and femininity on separate measurement scales, rather than opposite ends of the same continuum:

Low Femininity ⟵⟶ **High Femininity**

Low Masculinity ⟵⟶ **High Masculinity**

This produces a matrix with four outcomes, that is, the standard masculine and feminine, plus two new terms: androgynous and undifferentiated.

	Low Masculinity	High Masculinity
Low Femininity	Undifferentiated	Masculine
High Femininity	Feminine	Androgynous

Undifferentiated describes a pattern of lower scores both on measures of masculinity and femininity. Androgyny, by contrast, represents high scores both on measures of masculinity and femininity, not mid-way between, as often described in popular accounts, but high on both dimensions. Arguably, androgyny is another way of saying 'psychologically rounded'. However, despite best intentions, bias (of gender stereotypes) creep into respective measures for masculinity and femininity. Masculinity scores are better predictors of psychological well-being and self-determination. By contrast, the feminine traits incorporate child-like qualities and self-sacrifice. This is perhaps not surprising given the questionable methodologies used to devise psychometric tests for gender. The fundamental problem is that they are tautological. Masculinity is defined by items that men commonly support, and femininity from items that women commonly endorse. In effect, they are measuring adherence to social stereotypes.[53] Similar criticisms are levelled at Simon Baron-Cohen's *The Essential Brain*.[54]

In its earliest form, androgyny was criticized for being a bit 'warm and cuddly' and not addressing power imbalances between men and women.[55] Nevertheless, the concept of androgyny offers a leap in awareness, taking gender issues beyond the zero-sum game. The traits we label as masculine and feminine can be complementary rather than clashing, balancing rather than battling.

PSEUDOSCEPTICS AND THEIR DIFFERENCE DENIERS

Aside from evidence-based academic debate, the briefest of Internet searches will reveal challenges to the gender similarity hypothesis from self-styled sceptics. Some are well meaning and can provide a useful source of references for balanced critiques. However, there is a fine line between healthy scepticism and pseudoscepticism. The latter is often marked by virulent anti-feminism and accusations of 'difference denial' paired with their own denial of gender inequalities. Academics will often disagree with each other using language such as 'methodologically flawed' or 'erroneous conclusions'. Pseudosceptics will use words like 'claptrap' and 'garbage' or stronger, and it seems likely from a trawl of their website content that they set out with a priori assumptions (that is, they have pre-judged). Consequently, they only seek out information to confirm their schemata.[56]

CONCLUSIONS

This chapter explored how gender stereotypes are formed and maintained by various psychological mechanisms. It also examined the extent to which the biological sex differences (considered in Chapter 2) impact on our social and psychological selves. Considering the categories of femaleness and maleness, at many levels, the differences within the categories are often greater than the differences between categories. We might start off with small brain differences that are developed, nurtured and advanced by sociocultural expectations and behavioural differences. It's more plausible than the 'one-way arrow approach' of pop-psychology (and some academic psychology). Research evidence challenges the filter of biological essentialism. The similarities between men and women outweigh the differences. Furthermore, the differences are more often quantitative and not qualitative.

The next chapter considers the impact and implications of binary gender-role stereotypes. We know that one pay-off is cognitive economy, but what else? Are stereotypes a benign means by which we make sense of the world or are they harmful to our health, both physical and mental? It also considers other more far-reaching impacts.

4

THE IMPACT OF GENDER-ROLE STEREOTYPES

The goal of a zero-sum game of gender is to provide certainty, but what are the penalties? On the one hand, gender stereotypes are benignly descriptive, cognitively efficient devices that make the world a simpler place. However, on the other, they have a downside (or even a dark side). They can be malignly prescriptive and divisive. The previous chapter examined the blueprints for gender and began to consider some of the consequences for holding rigid gender-role stereotypes. In this chapter, we explore how gender stereotypes impact on our health and well-being and on our relations to society and the wider world. It also asks the fundamental question: Are gender stereotypes bad for us?

To draw together themes from previous chapters and move the discussion on, it helps to consider a more comprehensive definition of gender. It is

> the array of socially constructed roles and relationships, personality traits, attitudes, behaviours, values, relative power and influence that society ascribes to the two sexes on a differential basis . . . gender roles and characteristics do not exist in isolation, but are defined in relation to one another.[1]

THE MORBIDITY AND
MORTALITY PARADOX

Biologically, females have some advantage over males. As discussed in Chapter 2, the weaker Y chromosome means that males are more susceptible to a range of hereditary diseases and conditions. Stillbirth and infant mortality are also greater for males.[2] However, this biological difference does not translate into a clear-cut distinction. Whereas on average, males have a lower life expectancy, females tend to experience greater morbidity (poorer health). This is summed up in the epigram 'men die quicker, but women are sicker'.[3]

The female advantage in life expectancy is found throughout the world and has existed since the statistics began. The overall global average advantage is between three and four years.[4] However, this gap appears to be narrowing in industrialized countries.[5] There are enormous variations in life expectancy across the world, and between areas and communities within the same country. For instance, there is a 27-year difference in life expectancy between women in Australia and Zimbabwe (85 years versus 58 years). For men, the gap is narrower, at 23 years (80 years versus 57 years). There is only a one-year gap between the life expectancy of women and men in Zimbabwe (58 years versus 57 years). In Australia, the indigenous (Aboriginal) population has a shorter life expectancy by ten years compared with the non-indigenous population.[6]

Health inequalities between the sexes are the result of the interaction between biology and society (sex and gender) in terms of how society structures and influences our lives, and how we view the world. This means that biological differences can be amplified or suppressed and shape gender differences in attitudes to health.[7] For instance, women with chronic diseases and conditions are more likely to accept the complaint as part of themselves. In contrast, males are more apt to see it as a challenge to be overcome. Studies on gender differences in diabetes (in industrialized countries) reveal that females are generally more negative about coping with the condition, and experience more anxiety and depression than do males. However, men are also more likely to underestimate problems and long-term complications associated with diabetes.[8]

Males and females also have different experiences with healthcare. Women's reproductive health is also subject to more regular screenings (more intense medicalization), which might pick up other health conditions.[9] In medical settings (as in the feminine gender-role stereotype) females are socialized to be more compliant (in a male-dominated healthcare system) and to play what sociologist Talcott Parsons termed 'the sick role' – that is, 'play the patient'. This compliance might bring about a sense of *learned helplessness*[10] about health matters that leads to a sense of resignation, anxiety and depression around health. By contrast, men tend to wait until health problems become more severe – as part of the masculine gender stereotype men are less likely to seek help.[11] In contrast to the man-flu stereotype, the Monty Python scene in the Holy Grail film[12] rings true, where the knight with a severed arm insists on continuing to fight, protesting that 'it's just a flesh wound'.[13] Several studies have explored gender differences in 'the will to live' when faced with poor health or terminal conditions. Women appear to have the weaker desire to prolong life compared with men. Furthermore, living with a partner was a significant predictor of the will to live for men but not for women.[14] And who said that romance is dead?

Both men and women in long-term relationships live longer than do single people. They also tend to lose fewer days from work and visit the doctor less often. Some research has looked at the life expectancy of men and women in their mid-40s to mid-50s, with and without partners (that is, single, widowed or divorced). The results showed that out of men aged 45 to 54 years without a partner six out of 25 would die within a decade, compared to only three in 25 of men with a partner. However, for women aged 45 to 54 years without a partner, two in 25 would die within a decade compared to one in 25 of those with a partner. Figures for mental health also show a similar pattern. Although being in a relationship (married) is beneficial for both men and women, it has greater benefits for men.[15]

Work also is a key influence on health and wellbeing. Unemployed men are at an increased risk of psychological problems and early mortality. Work outside the home is related to improved health for women because of increased self-confidence and economic independence.[16]

LEADING CAUSES OF DEATH

Some health and well-being issues are more commonly associated with one gender. For example, dementia, depression and arthritis are more common in women. Men are more prone to lung cancer, cardiovascular disease and suicide.[17] However, the three leading causes of death in the Western world are cardiovascular disease (CVD), cancer, which we will cover in this section, and accidents, which we'll cover later in the chapter. All show marked gender differences.

Cardiovascular disease

CVD is the leading cause of death in industrialized nations, and although research does indicate gender differences, the patterns are not clear-cut. Although more women than men die from CVD, men are more likely to die younger, which may influence the impression that it is a man's disease. One factor implicated in gender differences is lifestyle risk. On average, men's diets, compared with women's diets, are higher in fat (particularly a higher ratio of saturated to polyunsaturated fats). Men's diets are also lower in vitamin C, and they smoke more. However, for exercise, which has a beneficial effect on health in general, men engage in more exercise compared with women. There has also been research into the role of hormones on CVD, particularly oestrogen. Some studies have indicated that it might have a protective effect for women; others have shown no effect. There has also been conflicting research on the impacts of hormone replacement therapy (HRT). Some studies have indicated a protective effect and others an increased risk of stroke for women (especially older women). The picture remains unclear.[18] What is clear is that gender stereotypes are implicated in the differential treatment of CVD. Models of CVD were developed using male patients. Women and men presenting with the same symptoms do not receive the same diagnosis and treatment. The belief that CVD is more of a male disease means that men are more likely to be referred for further tests and preventive treatment than are women. There is also a bias for ethnicity, which means, in the USA, creating a double jeopardy for African American women whose CVD symptoms are most likely to be overlooked.[19]

Cancer

Cancer is the second leading cause of deaths in the West. Overall, men have higher rates of death from cancer than do women. Lung cancer is the most prevalent form of cancer for both men and women and is highly correlated with smoking. There has been considerable debate on the disparity between funding for cancers, with breast cancer receiving substantially greater funding than does prostate cancer. However, evaluation of morbidity statistics reveals that aside from the obvious sex differences, there are marked age differences, and, on average, breast cancers occur younger in women than prostate cancer does in men. Therefore, it is argued that – in a limited resource system – the costs to society are greater for breast cancer. However, analysis suggests that both breast cancer and prostate cancer are over-funded in comparison to other cancers such as bladder, oesophageal, liver, oral, pancreatic, stomach and uterine.[20] Overall, it is notable that women have been very effective in mobilizing attention and charity activity for breast cancer, in a way that men are falling behind. There are also aspects of the masculine gender stereotype that get in the way, especially for younger men. First, males are socialized to be tough and not to look after their bodies as much as do females. Second, there is the issue of the permeability of the male body, the prospect of a rectal examination. Third, there is also the invasiveness of hidden cancers. Aggressive surgical treatments can lead to incontinence and impotence, severely degrading the quality of life. A lot of attention has focused on the devastating impact on femininity of breast cancer, but not so much on the loss of manhood represented by these harsh treatments – because men are just supposed to 'tough it out'. A significant medical breakthrough could provide a vital change in the treatment for (and attitudes to) prostate cancer. It involves a drug made from deep-sea bacteria, injected into the bloodstream and activated in the prostate by laser beams. This has the potential to be a real 'game-changer' for men's health.[21]

STEREOTYPES, EATING AND EXERCISING

The two main factors implicated in better health are eating and exercise. Both show gender differences. On average, women are more apt to eat healthier diets, and men are more likely to exercise. This is one example of where androgyny would be good for our health. However, the effects of stereotypes are revealed in the extremes of behaviour.

Both stereotypes involve self-evaluation to some external standard, for men it is usually other men. Women's magazines also focus on 'what men want' of women. Overall, the theme is that men should make themselves bigger and women should make (keep) themselves smaller. As 'slimness' is part of idealized femininity – in the West – eating disorders are also more common in women. This combines with the stereotype that females are supposed to be less active than males and therefore don't need so much energy (food). Not surprisingly then, in industrialized countries, gender plays an important factor in determining risk factors for eating disorders such as anorexia nervosa and bulimia nervosa. One explanation is the emphasis placed on 'ideal' female body shape in Western society, often linked to unrealistic representations in fashion and lifestyle magazines. A key aspect of the feminine stereotype is the desire to please others. Dieting might be used to improve body image and self-esteem. Among males, troubled eating is more common among sports competitors and gay men. Around 90% of those treated for eating disorders are female. However, given men are reluctant to seek medical treatment generally, the figure for males might be an underestimation.[22]

The masculine gender stereotype and muscularity often go together. Young boys are often encouraged to display their muscles, that is, their biceps. In *Male Impersonators*, journalist and gender theorist, Mark Simpson argues that in the pursuit of bigger and bigger bodies, some men are putting themselves at risk with over-training and extreme diets.

In cutting, almost Freudian analysis he suggests that bodybuilding is about men transforming themselves into living hard and veined phallic symbols.[23] The contradiction is that the side effects of steroid over-use include reduced sperm count, infertility, erectile dysfunction, increased risk of prostate cancer, shrunken testicles and breast development.[24] It is definitely an example of where bigger is not better. Big muscles and good health are not necessarily synonymous.

Revealingly, in symbolic terms, men refer to their biceps as 'guns'. In real-life terms firearms (and violence) have a devastating impact on life expectancy for men.

UNTIMELY ENDS AND GENDER

Nothing illustrates the effects of the 'pillars of manhood' (anti-femininity, superiority, self-reliance and power) like the statistics for death rates for accidents and violence.[25] Reviewing mortality rates in the USA from accidents and violence in 2013, there are stark gender differences, across three ethnic groups: European Americans, African Americans and Hispanic Americans. Overall, males are about three times more likely to die from violent deaths than are females. The figures hold throughout a lifetime but are more pronounced in earlier years. Men tend to behave in ways that increase risks, such as higher alcohol use, dangerous driving and lower frequency of seat belt use, higher occupational hazards, acts of physical aggression and illegal activities.[26]

Men are just over two and half times more likely to die in motor vehicle accidents than are females, and this figure is similar across all ethnic groups. For deaths from firearms-related injuries, there are notable differences among ethnic groups. Among European Americans, men are five-and-a-half times more likely to die from firearms than are women, African American men are almost ten times more likely and Hispanic American men are 14 times more likely. There are also notable gender differences in homicide statistics. European American men are about two-and-a-half times more likely to be murdered than are women. For Hispanic American men it is five times more likely, and African American men are almost seven times more likely. Aspiring to be 'the big wheel' has devastating consequences in a zero-sum game.

Suicide statistics also reveal gender differences. Although women are more likely to attempt suicide, men are more prone to succeed. The main reason for the gender difference is that men tend to choose methods that are more likely to be lethal, such as guns, hanging and jumping from high places. By contrast, women are more apt to choose 'gentler' methods such as drug overdoses.[27] It is plausible, in keeping with stereotypes, that women consider how their bodies will be found, and consider the feelings of others.

The statistics for suicide attempts in LGBT sub-populations indicate additional pressures of not fitting into a binary world. Whereas in the USA, for the general population, the suicide-attempt rate is around 4.6%, it rises steeply for LGBT people. For LGBT people it is between 10% and 20%. However, among trans and gender-nonconforming people it is 41%. The highest figure is for trans men at 46%. The higher categories include age (younger are more at risk) and ethnicity (people of colour are more at risk than White people).[28] As we have seen in previous chapters, the world is viewed from a male perspective and therein lies the imbalance of power, but as the above figures have shown, the division is not 'straight down the middle'.

PRIVILEGE AND PATRIARCHY

Gender-role stereotypes and inequalities need to be understood in the context of a system of power-structured relationships.

The gender gap

According to feminist scholar and activist Kate Millett, gender is a system in which 'sex is a status category with political implications' – this is *patriarchy*,[29] one where men have the privilege of power, often referred to as 'male privilege'. The word 'privilege' – a schema in itself – is often tossed into discussions like a rhetorical grenade. Dividing societies along gender lines leads to inequalities and discrimination for women *as a group* and, usually, in the allocation of scarce resources, it is men *as a group* who benefit most.[30] Performance artist, Laurie Anderson commenting, acerbically, on the gender pay gap (in industrialized countries): 'For every dollar a man makes a woman makes 63 cents. Now, fifty years ago that was 62 cents. So, with that kind of luck, it'll be the year 3,888, before we make a buck'.[31] Comparing the median earnings of men and women in full-time employment, globally, women earn 18% less than men. However, the gap increases when we consider how work is divided along gender lines – usually as productive labour or reproductive labour. Productive labour is income-generating employment (typically outside the home). Reproductive labour is that which is performed in the home, that is, reproducing the conditions for survival, such as food preparation, housework and childcare. Customarily, in both industrialized and developing countries, women spend more time in reproductive, volunteer and unpaid labour, whereas men spend more time in productive, paid work.[32] Work designated 'women's work' is consistently taken for granted and undervalued.

Patriarchal dividend

The surplus of resources – the advantage to men *as a group* from maintaining an equal gender order – is called the *patriarchal dividend*. Apart from money, other benefits of the gender system include authority, respect, service, housing, access to institutional power, emotional support, sex and control over one's own body (and the bodies of others).[33] However, how much men benefit depends on their position in the social order. Some get a lot of it, others less and some get none. Kate Bornstein refers to a gender power pyramid with a few, unimaginably wealthy White men at the top.[34] 'Privilege' is often used in a binary way but there is a vast difference between a double-digit billionaire male and his male employee on a minimum wage, zero hours contract. The patriarchal dividend is not always all about men. Some women participate in the patriarchal dividend too, through inheritance or marriage. Trade in domestic labour has helped support middle-class women's careers without requiring their middle-class male partners to do more of their share of domestic labour.[35] Social psychologist Roy Baumeister argues that in examining the system, the mistake is to look only at the male-dominated top and ignore the bottom of the pyramid at the 'failures', or rather those failed by the system. Men make up the majority (93% in the USA) of the prison population. Men make up most political prisoners around the world, those killed in battle, the homeless, and those doing the most dangerous jobs.[36] Baumeister argues that as well as the exploitation of women, the system also thrives on the expendability of men.[37] It is a high-risk, 'who dares win' system and the rewards are great, such as power, wealth, authority, respect, autonomy, control over one's own body (and over others), sex and so on – in short, all the needs (motivation) encompassed in the masculine gender.

Risky business

The patriarchal dividend is the primary stake in the binary gender system and one that makes patriarchy worth defending.[38] Most cultures tend to use men for these high-risk, high-payoff slots much more than women. The message to men is: prove you are a man, take risks and die trying. The result is that some men reap big rewards while others have their lives ruined or cut short. To illustrate the expendability of men, Baumeister reviews the survival rates for the Titanic marked by its 'women and children first' approach. He comments that the richest men had a lower survival rate than the poorest women (34% versus 46%).[39] Further analysis of the figures shows that the overall survival rate for men was 20%, compared with 52% for children and 74% for women. Men in First Class were twice as likely to be saved as men in Third Class (32% versus 16%). Comparing figures for the crew, almost 87% of women were saved compared with 20% of men.[40] Baumeister argues, contentiously, that wombs are more valuable than penises in evolutionary terms; hence 'most cultures keep their women out of harm's way (albeit oppressively) while using men for risky jobs'.[41]

Rape and sexual assault

The so-called protection for women comes at a cost, particularly in relation to power over women's bodies. On average, about one-third of women worldwide report physical and/or sexual violence by an intimate partner.[42] In England and Wales, 11 adults are raped every hour – around 85,000 women and 12,000 men per year. Approximately 90% of those who are raped know the perpetrator prior to the offence. When all sexual assaults are included (such as unwanted touching and indecent exposure), the figure rises to almost half a million adults. One in five women aged 16 to 59 years has experienced some form of sexual violence (since the age of 16). Overall, only about 15% of those who experience sexual violence choose to report it to the police.[43] Figures from the USA indicate that one-half (but up to two-thirds) of transgender people are sexually abused or assaulted, or physically assaulted at some point in their lives.[44] In a 2013 United Nations-funded survey of more than 10,000 men, the most common reasons for rape included sexual entitlement, seeking of entertainment and as a punishment. Associated factors included low empathy, alcohol use, and masculinities emphasizing heterosexual performance, dominance over women and participation in gangs.[45] In some analyses, it has been suggested that rather than seen as pathological, perpetrators of gang rape see it as way of proving themselves to the gang. It is also viewed as a way of creating unity with the gang (and a fear of being ostracized), part of developing and proving their masculinity, personal and collective pride in reducing another being to nothingness.[46] It is also a way for men to be naked with each other, in a sexualized environment, and still abide by the 'no cissy stuff' rule – although they probably don't see it that way.

Sexual entitlement of men is enshrined in pop-psychology books bought and read by women, such as *Mars and Venus in the Bedroom* (mentioned in Chapter 3). Women (in heterosexual relationships) who are not in the mood for sex are guilt-tripped into letting their partners have a 'quickie'. Analyzing another self-help book (*Why Men Don't*

Iron), psychologists Wendy and Rex Stainton-Rogers argue that 'it comes dangerously close to suggesting that men who rape cannot help it' because of 'a testosterone-fuelled, irresistible urge'.[47] It is not difficult to see Bem's gender lenses at work here. Analysis of gang rapes indicates that the motivations are linked to the pillars of manhood (from Chapter 3). In academic terms, it is defined as *hegemonic masculinity*, one that sanctions male dominance in society and justifies the subordination of women (and other 'lesser' men). Many self-help books (more harm than help) prize this form of masculinity and find ways to work around it with their feminine wiles and trade-offs. Other ways of being a man are disparaged.

ATTITUDES

Our pattern-seeking brain by which we form and maintain gender-role stereotypes and schemata is perhaps typified by the idiom 'birds of a feather flock together'. In Chapter 3 we considered the concept of authoritarianism (and its link with binary thinking) and the functions of attitudes (instrument, knowledge, values and ego-defensive). Put this together with the concept of in-groups, out-groups (us versus them) and halo effects. All of this explains how some people take it personally when others do not behave to the same standards. This can have far-reaching implications in that if an individual holds 'hierarchic, status conscious, authoritarian, power based and rigid attitudes' within the family, then he or she is expected to hold similar views in other relationships but also towards social and political issues.

Many psychological studies have found a correlation between it and traditional gender roles. People with high scores in authoritarianism tend to hold more narrowly defined gender roles with attractiveness based on conventional masculine and feminine ideals. This also influences on romantic relationships and lifestyle goals.[48] Opposition to trans people's civil rights is correlated with authoritarianism, heterosexism, a belief that there are only two sexes, beliefs that gender is biologically based and heterosexism. Psychologist Adrian

Furnham describes a list of characteristics that comprise authoritarianism. These include conventionalism, acceptance of authority, a tendency to condemn anyone who violates the norms and rejection of weakness or sentimentality. In addition, there are also links to categorical (binary) thinking, a preoccupation with dominance (power and toughness) over others, exaggerated concerns for proper sexual conduct including homophobia, generalized feelings of hostility and anger and a tendency to project inner emotions and impulses outward (projection).[49]

High scores on authoritarianism were related to traditional gender-role identity and attitudes, rating political events concerning women as less important, and rating feminists and women as having relatively more power and influence in society. Authoritarianism was also related to the expression of anti-abortion views in essays and using arguments based on conventional morality, submission to authority, and punitiveness toward women seeking abortions. Finally, high scores on authoritarianism were related to participating in pro-life rallies and not participating in pro-choice and women's issues meetings.[50] In another study, researchers found that relative to women, men reported higher levels of homophobia, ethnocentrism and right-wing authoritarianism. Gender differences in homophobia were also conditioned by dismissive-avoidant attachment styles, in particular, a fear of intimacy seemed to contribute to homophobic attitudes found among heterosexual men.[51]

The film *Pleasantville* is a visually stunning tale of the political and sexual awakening in a small 1950s town. According to its director, Gary Ross, the theme driving the narrative is that 'personal repression gives rise to larger political oppression'. He adds 'when we're afraid of certain things in ourselves or we're afraid of change, we project those fears on to other things, and a lot of very ugly social situations can develop'.[52] Although often referred to as the *authoritarian personality*, this individualizes the issue. The cluster of tendencies, characteristics, attributes, and opinions that make up this cognitive organization is intelligible in a limited-resources, zero sum-game, binary system.

CONCLUSIONS

Gender stereotypes may well be a way to structure the world, but it does not mean they are good for us – being 'real men' or 'real women' may actually be bad for our health. From morbidity to mortality, from the health inequalities and biases within the system to economic and sexual violence, this brief review indicates that we need to question the binary system. Biological inevitably on its own cannot explain the differences; we must look more closely at the societal roles and factors. Rigid adherence to (stereotypical) gender roles also narrows human experience and hinders opportunity, and creates barriers to leading a fuller life. To some degree, we are all held hostage by gender-role stereotypes and taunted by the spectre of the expectations of unattainable ideals and hidden biases. It is not surprising that researchers are increasingly attributing both physical and mental health problems to rigid gender roles.

Chapter 5 takes a lighter look at stories that inform gender roles as well as looking at alternative ways of doing gender – steps on the way to a new paradigm.

5

GENDER STORIES, BACKWARDS, FORWARDS AND SIDEWAYS

By way of an antidote to the impersonal world of statistics and the dark side of gender-role stereotypes (in Chapter 4), this chapter begins an excursion into the stories we tell about gender. Here we contemplate how we use human creativity (and psychology) to consider alternative gender schemata in which we might thrive. This first half of the chapter discusses the lasting effects of Judaeo-Christian scripture on gender-role stereotypes and binary thinking. It also explores other stories, such as fairy tales, science fiction and re-readings of cultural history, all of which can impact on our gender schemata. The second half of the chapter considers ways forward for a new psychology of gender.

MEANING-MAKING AND GENDER

Gender adds a great deal to cultural richness.[1] Chances are it plays an integral part in your favourite works of art, such as books, plays, poems, songs, paintings, films and television programmes. Throughout history, art has deployed gender in ways that are fun, entertaining or thought provoking.[2] From Shakespeare's plays to the films of John Waters, from Japanese Noh to British Pantomime, from Glam Rock to Hip Hop, from New Romantics to Punk, from Yaoi[3] to fan fiction, gender is a vital ingredient. Human creativity imbues our lives, and our schemata, with colour and meaningfulness.

We are all storytellers. We all have life stories. Your story is not just a linear narrative. You edit and construct it to convey a sense of who you are, your psychology, your identity. Your story is also open to different interpretations by others, in terms of how you fit into their stories. Sociologist Michael Mulkay argues that 'every "social action" and every "cultural product" or "text" has to be treated as a source or an opportunity for creating multiple meaning, or further texts'.[4] Psychologists Wendy and Rex Stainton-Rogers contend that 'research reports are the products of human meaning-making, as much are films, fictions and fantasies'.[5] Common sense, pop-psychology and academic psychology all tell different stories about gender. This book began with an allusion to dystopian science fiction short story *Minority Report* which tells of advanced pre-cognitive crime detection systems. Gender is also about having our lives mapped out before we have lived them, and as much about self-identity, just as with science fiction, it is about making sense of our relationship with 'aliens and others'.

We begin with an early example of meaning-making that still influences the social and political world today.

COSMOLOGY AND AMBIGUITY

Classics scholar Richard Hoffman defines a cosmology, in its broadest sense, as a culturally specific account of how the universe came about.[6] We might think of a cosmology as an over-arching meta-schema. The earliest cosmologies were religious accounts whose primary purpose was to help people make sense of the human experience (and their place in the universe). They imposed a structure that included the roles and functions of the culture's inhabitants and their relationship to each other and to outsiders. This encompassed gender roles and attitudes to sex and sexuality. English and American literature scholar Elaine Scarry argues that Judaeo-Christian scripture can be credited with 'sponsoring a civilization to a degree shared by no other isolated verbal text'.[7] Its influences are still detectable in Western psychology, psychiatry, medicine and the law. Canon law (church law) became criminal law, that is, sins (against the divine order) became crimes against the state.[8]

It helps to distinguish between two types of cosmology (there goes another binary). There are monotheistic cosmologies such as Judaism, Christianity and Islam, which have only one god, and polytheistic cosmologies such as Hinduism, which has many. These types of cosmologies offer distinctive ways of structuring the world. Monotheism leans towards a monochrome (binary) view and polytheist towards a polychrome view. Monotheistic (one-god) cosmologies describe rigid boundaries between the realms of the mortal and the divine, and regarding the roles and functions of people.

The creation myth in Hebrew scripture begins with a series of binaries: form/void, night/day, good/bad, man/woman and so on. By contrast, a polytheistic (many-god) cosmology is marked by less rigid boundaries between mortal and divine realms, with frequent interaction, even sexual intercourse, between the two. Gods in polytheistic religions had female gods and gods with the physical anatomy of both sexes (intersex). Furthermore, sex would not be considered a negative force, as in monotheistic religions, but may be used as part of a sacred ritual, as with ancient Egyptian and Canaanite religions. This leads to differences in the way sex and gender are organized in everyday life. One-god, gender schemata are more likely to offer a dichotomy of male versus female. Furthermore, the system does not allow for anomalies or grey areas (as in Judaeo-Christian scripture). There can be no blending or blurring. Anthropologist Mary Douglas in *Purity and Danger*[9] argues that the main theme running throughout the Old Testament Holiness Code[10] is the integrity of boundaries. Distinctions between the sacred and the profane became paramount for the Israelite identity so that 'everything that suggests ambiguity and the breaking down of distinctions is forbidden'.[11] The Laws of Western Thought and Bem's gender lenses (biological essentialism, gender polarity and androcentrism), discussed in Chapter 3 would be at home here. By contrast, a polytheistic gender-schema system allows a more relaxed approach to gender ambiguity and anomaly. In modern-day terms, they might be described as genderqueer.

Another important issue is how a cosmology deals with the gods from other religions. In Judaeo-Christian, one-god schema, gods from neighbouring religions were treated as hostile and incorporated into alternative names for evil/the devil (for example Beelzebub). The fertility goddess Asherah/Astarte former consort of the Hebrew God (Yahweh) was thoroughly excised and even changed sex. Her shrines (sacred groves) were destroyed (Deuteronomy 12: 3–4), her name was rendered in Greek translations to mean just 'groves' and she appears to have lived out the rest of her life as a male daemon, Astaroth, the Great Duke of Hell.[12] Because polytheism was a feature of early civilizations, popular wisdom would have it that monotheism represents an advance. In the case of Judaeo-Christian evolution, this 'progress' involved the erasure of the goddess. This contrasts with polytheistic religions that would find it easier to incorporate other gods into their pantheon. For instance, Native American belief systems would have had no problem in accepting Jesus Christ as a god but did have problems accepting that there was only one God.[13]

The shift towards monotheism (in Judaeo-Christian scripture) meant 'spelling things out' to establish clear boundaries; this involved a whole new raft of laws to manage the ambiguities. The Holiness Code deals with 'pollution from forbidden unions'.[14] This included everything from food, to planting a field, to animals used for a plough, to clothes, to cross-dressing, to sex. In an environment perceived to be hostile, the laws were to ensure the integrity and survival of a cultural identity, one that was distinct from polytheistic Canaanites and the Egyptians. Douglas argues that unclean (dirty) just means 'matter out of place' in the scheme of things. I tested this idea in my research and found that participants rated sex acts that did not conform to traditional gender roles (and the people who did them) dirtier than those that did.[15]

The monotheistic/polytheistic binary split of cultures cannot be fully supported. For instance, in Ancient Greece, there were distinct gender divisions and roles with women not recognized as citizens. In this instance, we could argue that polytheism offered a broader behavioural range for masculine identity, particularly regarding sexual expression. However, in analysis of Native American cultures, attitudes to (third gender) two-spirit people changed with the introduction of Christianity – from reverence to shame. Different ways of expressing gender in indigenous cultures encountered by European conquerors were religious fervour and suppressed and punished with extreme brutality and violence. It is also notable that in many older travel accounts of other cultures (ethnographic studies), 'men of colour' were feminized generally, in comparison to White, European standards of the day.[16] There is little in the way of empirical support for Hoffman's analysis. However, I did work with a student on their final year dissertation, which offers tentative support. It examined monotheistic and polytheistic attitudes among Asian students towards homosexual and heterosexual behaviour. Participants completed several psychometric measures, including negative attitudes to homosexuality (homophobia), religiosity and monotheism. Participants were divided into two groups: monotheist (Sikhs and Muslims) and polytheist (Hindus). Group membership was confirmed by scores on the monotheism scale. Despite significantly higher scores on religiosity, the polytheist group scored significantly lower on the measure of negative attitudes to homosexuality.[17]

SOUL MATES, OTHER HALVES AND PLURAL PRONOUNS

Biblical creationist stories still hold sway today and are often invoked to justify fixed gender roles and (negative) attitudes to sexuality. Reference to Adam and Eve is the scriptural metaphor for Bem's gender lenses.[18] However, the journey from polytheism left some interesting artefacts in these accounts. In the Biblical creation story, God was translated from the word Elohim, which is actually a masculine plural (literally 'the gods' – which could comprise a group of gods, goddesses and other deities). The Book of Genesis gives two accounts of the creation of humans. Genesis 1 verse 26–27 (Revised Standard Version) reads 'Then [the gods] said, "Let us make [humans] in our image, after our likeness" . . . 27 So [the gods] created [humans] in his own image, in the image of [the gods] he created him; male and female he created them'.[19] This implies that, in this story, original humans were either psychologically or physically androgynous (or intersexed). Today, many genderqueer people have abandoned the singular masculine and feminine pronouns and instead refer to themselves using the plural 'them' and 'they'.

In Plato's *Symposium*, from Classical Greece, comic playwright Aristophanes entertains at a party with a tale explaining why two people feel whole when they find love. The story goes that in primal times people had doubled bodies, with faces and limbs turned outward from one another. There were three sexes: a double-male (descended from the Sun), a double-female (descended from the Earth) and a half-male-half-female (descended from the Moon).[20] These primal humans tried to scale Mount Olympus to set upon the gods. So, as a punishment, Zeus chopped them in half (vertically) creating two separate beings. Their fate was to run around looking for their other halves (soul mates) to recover their original nature. Returning to the Book of Genesis, there is a second account of the creation of Adam and Eve, where Adam is created first, and, as common knowledge would have it, Eve is fashioned from Adam's rib (Genesis 2 verses 21–22). First, Adam is a general term for human, meaning 'red earth'. Second, the word tsela is translated as 'rib' on this single occasion, although 40 times elsewhere in the Bible the same word is rendered as 'side'.[21] So, by this reading, the gods split the first human in half, offering a more egalitarian version of the creation myth.

THE CHALICE AND THE BLADE

In *The Chalice and the Blade*,[22] historian and systems scientist Riane Eisler reviews a broad range of evidence throughout history, much of it focused on the Minoan civilization on Crete. She claims that, in the prehistory of humans, partnership used to be the norm. Much of the material centres on goddess worship and cultures and civilizations that emphasized consensus. Eisler presents two contrasting models of human history.[23]

Contemporary world societies are based on domination and are symbolized by the power of the blade. These are marked by

- A structure of rigid top-down rankings – hierarchies of domination maintained through physical, psychological and economic control.
- The rigid ranking of one-half of humanity over the other half.
- Culturally accepted abuse and violence.
- Beliefs that relations of domination and submission are inevitable, normal and even moral.

The alternative model highlights a society symbolized by the chalice, marked by

- A democratic and egalitarian structure.
- Equal partnership between women and men.
- Abuse and violence not culturally accepted (that is, not institutionalized or idealized).
- Beliefs about human nature that support empathic and mutually respectful relations.

Eisler's argument challenges the schemata that asymmetrical social structures are inevitable. She coins the term 'gylany', which is made up of 'gy' from 'gyno' (woman) and 'an' from 'andro' (man). The 'l' in the middle of the word represents the Greek verb 'lyo' or 'lyein' meaning 'to solve or resolve'. The aspiration is that just as many relationships in the West have moved to partnership models, so societies could in the future be based on consensus-based gylany again, too.

FAIRY TALES AND GENDER

In *The Uses of Enchantment*,[24] psychologist and psychoanalyst Bruno Bettelheim discusses the meaning and importance of fairy tales, including early versions of familiar favourites. These stories helped children make sense of the world and cope with confusing emotions. Many fairy tales contained coded messages about sex and gender. They invariably involved themes of chivalrous princes rescuing beautiful but hapless princesses. You don't need to be a psychoanalyst to discern the significance of the pubescent Little Red Riding Hood being warned not to stray off the path or else she might fall prey to the blood-thirsty wolf.

Over the years these stories have been modified and sanitized and so have lost much of their significance. Bettelheim recounts an earlier version of *Jack and the Beanstalk*. In *Jack and His Bargains*, the problems of moving from boyhood to manhood are clearer, and, surprisingly, offer a different view of the traditional phallocentric male gender-role stereotype. At the start of the story, Jack is described as wild and of no use to his father and his family who have fallen on hard times. Jack is sent to the fair to sell a cow. On the way, he meets a man who offers to exchange it for a magic stick that Jack can use to defeat his enemies. All he needs to do is shout the magic words 'Up stick and at it'. Not surprisingly his father is angry and fetches a stick to beat Jack who calls upon his magic stick and beats the father. Jack is then charged with going to sell two more cows, meets the same man on the road and comes home with a bee (that sings beautiful songs) one time and a fiddle (a violin that plays marvellous tunes) the other. As with many fairy tales, there is a quest for the heart of a princess. Jack achieves this by lots of superior 'stick-work', but also through humour and a display of sexual self-restraint. The bee in the story might represent the sweetness of life or hard work, and the violin might be artistic achievement. Overall the story emphasizes that the 'stick' is not enough. The story begins with an adolescent preoccupation with the phallic supremacy and in maturity ends with a broader range of values and abilities. In terms of *Maslow's Hierarchy of Needs* – a theory of motivation – musical talent and humour are of a higher order than are safety, security needs and basic physiological survival needs. Moving from the bottom to the top of the pyramid, the needs become less about survival and more about psychological growth.[25]

SCIENCE FICTION AND OTHER HUMAN MEANING-MAKING

Science fiction – although often typically reflecting the status quo of heroes and damsels in distress – offers the possibility of exploring social and linguistic conventions beyond the mundane.[26] Stainton-Rogers and Stainton-Rogers identify several writers, notably in the 1960s through to the 1980s, who attempted to explore, in the science fiction genre, taken-for-granted assumptions around sex and gender (including personal pronouns). In *The Left Hand of Darkness* (1969), Ursula Le Guin explores a planet on which its inhabitants are androgynous and asexual who periodically and temporarily become males and females. In the books of Mary Gentle – *Golden Witchbreed* (1983) and *Ancient Light* (1987) – the alien race socializes its children in a gender-neutral way. Raising gender-aschematic children was the main aim of Sandra Bem's work.

With the proliferation of communication and information technology, no longer is our world view determined by the people who control the written word. In Western cultures, we can mix-and-match information sources, and in particular, the Internet has democratized knowledge (for those who can get unhindered access to it). It offers opportunities to create and consider alternate versions of reality, which has a mediating effect on our understanding of gender and sexuality. Some of its content seeks to cement the traditional binaries, and other seeks to up-end accepted 'wisdom'. In the cyber-world, we can all pass as 'aliens and others'. Through fan fiction, we can create our own narratives for fictional characters such as the love-hate relationship between Magneto and Professor Xavier in the X-men. Other stories centre on imagined intimate relationships between the actors who play them[27] in scenes reminiscent of Japanese Yaoi – comic books about male relationships written for a teenage female audience.

In something of a contradiction, advances in *digital* technology have created a platform to explore *analogue* views of identity. At its best, the Internet offers limitless opportunities to test the boundaries of gender identity and relationships. At its worst, it descends into a battleground of polarized, blade-wielding cliques claiming to be 'on the right side of history'. So, where do we go from here?

TOWARDS A NEW PSYCHOLOGY OF GENDER

Are we on the brink of a new gender paradigm, are we tinkering with the old one, or are we living in a new paradigm? Are we moving backwards, forwards or sideways?

In the first half of the chapter, we considered an unlikely collection of stories. Each one highlights a feature of the challenges faced in rewriting gender. The distinction between monotheism and polytheism is similar to the tensions between binary gender and gender queerness. For some, it's a step forward, and for others a descent into chaos. The impish rewriting of the creation myth combining Adam, Eve and Aristophanes represents a challenge to androcentrism (and a reminder that gender should be fun, too). The early version of the *Jack and the Beanstalk* embodies a (less phallocentric) challenge to the masculine gender stereotype. What scripts can we offer men other than winners and losers, tough guys and wimps and that come at such a great human cost? *The Chalice and the Blade* metaphor provides an alternative model for moving forward. Do we listen or tell? Do we use consensus or domination? Bygone worlds or the otherworldliness of science fiction (and fan-fiction) stories offer the opportunity to consider alternatives, including the effects of language, such as personal pronouns. In a post-ladies-and-gentlemen world, are we he/she/ze/xe/they, him/her/hir/xir/them or xem?

In many ways, the contests in gender politics parallel changes in psychology as a discipline, particularly with the challenges of feminism.

Rehabilitating the malestream

Psychology as a discipline has responded, often reluctantly, to address many of the biases it had consciously or unconsciously imported from the 'real' world. The mainstream view is often called the 'malestream' view. Earlier attempts focused on tweaking the framework to include women (and alienated 'others'), still left a broadly androcentric discipline that focused on masculinity (and heterosexuality) as the default (and often invisible) benchmark.[28] 'Women's issues' remained a postscript. Feminist psychology offers a fundamental challenge, giving centre stage to 'new ways of knowing' and meaning-making. This included a challenge to what constitutes knowledge (epistemology), a challenge to the methods and approaches psychologists used to gain evidence (modes of enquiry) and a challenge to the topics and issues studied (subject matter).[29] This has paved the way for LGBTQI+ perspectives on psychology, offering radically different understandings of what it means to be a woman, a man or 'something completely different'. This includes the work that tells us that there are multiple masculinities, female masculinities and people living outside, beyond or across gender categories.[30]

However, pop-psychology has not kept pace and still champions the 'role, pole and hole' model of gender with planetary metaphors less enlightened (and inclusive) compared with those of the Ancient Greeks. Even neuroscience tells us that our brains are more mosaic than monochrome. Stainton-Rogers and Stainton-Rogers argue that it is 'all very well celebrating some sort of postmodern carnival'; but, 'If everything is in flux – if we are living in a world of new men, new women and new relationships – then is it possible to have any idea of where we are going, or . . . where we should be going?'[31] What are the larger impacts of gender? More than a way for us to view our bodies, our individual psychology and our relations, there are much broader implications. If we can't use stereotypes then how can we make sense of the world, what will be the impact of sexual attraction, will we all become 'neutroids' and usher in the end of humanity? More important than what happens in the future is what is going on now. Are we taking everyone with us or do some get left behind? Talk about male privilege can obscure the possibility that it is not just men that are affected by changes in gender relations. As Connell and Pearse warn, it's a threat to many women, too, as 'Impending changes can upset people's cherished image of themselves, assumptions about personal relationships, their social embodiment and their habits of everyday conduct'.[32] A new paradigm needs to be fit for purpose and not include new ways of oppressing those oppressed by the old-world view.

Can we move beyond binary gender?

As children we begin with no notion of gender, our views become polarized (around the time we accept gender constancy) and this rigid view relaxes, probably more so for females than for males.[33] From adolescence, we set about the project of 'finding ourselves' and carving out our own identity – depending on our circumstances. There are wide differences within and between cultures in opportunities they offer for gender conformity and gender variability. In Chapter 3, we began to consider the concept of androgyny, the idea that we can simultaneously embody strong agentic and instrumental ('masculine') and expressive and nurturing ('feminine') traits. However, as discussed, early conceptualizations of androgyny still made a masculine/feminine distinction, and the masculine qualities were deemed more positive. Androgyny also fails to address power imbalances and material disadvantages (or patriarchal dividend).[34] Money and power tend to colour gender.

There have been other attempts to re-imagine gender categories, such as Martine Rothblatt's *The Apartheid of Sex* which offers a colour-coded paradigm for gender and sexual identity. Rothblatt describes it as a 'deconstruction of sexual identity into objective, ungenitally infected elements'.[35] This 'chromatic lexicon' is achieved by the interaction of three primary coloured elements of identity. Thus, activeness is coded yellow, passivity is blue, and eroticism is coded red. Individuals rank themselves on three seven-point scales, which provide 343 unique chromatic gender/sexual identities. In effect, it is a sexualized androgyny, and in practice, it is doubtful that system would overcome the pervasiveness of gender stereotypes with masculinity associated with aggression and femininity with passivity. It might also fall foul of the double standard in attitudes to sexual behaviour. It also leaves us with lots of different colours with no real framework of how they fit together.

Yes, they are all on the colour wheel but how do we make sense of it in everyday life? Furthermore, as with androgyny, it obscures the power differences of age, class and other social and cultural factors.[36] Adding a scale for power and another for patriarchal dividend would 'muddy the waters'. Despite its limitations, Rothblatt's polychromatic system can still be useful in sparking a debate around sex and gender.

Much of Sandra Bem's work focused on the prospect of raising gender aschematic children. The challenge is to avoid interpreting children's behaviour through adult (binary) filters. A boy might play with dolls, and a girl might play with cars. One or both might grow up to be parents. One or both might grow up to have driving licences. They are not necessarily signs of gender confusion. They might just be playing. Sometimes the dressing up box is just the dressing up box. All children at some point hold an amorphous view of gender. In a polarized gender world, it would be surprising if no one ever thought what it was like 'on the other side'. What we know is that as adults, people in gender unconventional jobs tend to express non-traditional gender schemata.[37] Part of this is recognizing that different ways of doing gender might be appropriate in different circumstances. An individual might be nurturing and rational in one situation, assertive and sensitive in another.

According to Connell and Pearse, instead of either/or gender we 'get a picture of psychological gender differences and similarities not as fixed, age-old constants of the species, but as the changing products of the active responses people make to a complex and changing social world'.[38] On this view, androgyny could just be another way of saying 'psychological roundedness',[39] fit for a modern world. It might simply be about cognitive flexibility and adaptability. The question is how this infiltrates the androcentric workplace.

Gylany in psychology

The concept of *emotional intelligence* (EI) is a contested topic among researchers. Its proponents proclaim it as the panacea for all ills and positively correlated with better social relations, more successful relations, less interpersonal aggression, better academic achievement, better negotiating abilities, better psychological well-being, higher life satisfaction, higher self-esteem, lower levels of insecurity and lower levels of depression. It is negatively correlated with poor health choices and behaviours. They also decry the most ubiquitous form – arguing that it is pop-psychology.[40] However, Goleman's version has found favour in the business world, and it is now seen as the 'must have' for all good leaders. His five-construct model can be divided into two categories. The personal competencies are self-awareness, self-regulation and motivation. The social competencies are social skills and empathy.[41] Taken together, with a dose of goal-setting, we have an approximation to androgyny. There is much research to be done in this relatively new concept in psychology. However, it appears to offer the signs of a more level playing field for women in the business world. So much so that Daniel Goleman claims that although data are emerging that show a leadership advantage for women, 'the smart way to use this finding lies in spotting the right women for leadership'. And he adds,

> The key phrase in interpreting these findings is 'on average.' Any broad comparison of men and women on a behavior like emotional intelligence yields two largely overlapping bell curves, with women's average ratings higher than men's. But because these curves overlap that means any given man might be as effective in, say, achieving goals or teamwork as any woman.[42]

So, the byword is 'the right women, but any given man'. The significant shift here is that the traditionally masculine trait of leadership has been redefined in a way that is 'more chalice and less blade'. The values and the goals have shifted towards gylany and qualities traditionally categorized as feminine are now linked with success in the world.

There is a general move towards a more inclusive psychology, and one approach, positive psychology, is charged with research aspects of human psychology that are more positive, in a universal sense. It is defined as 'the scientific study of the strengths that enable individuals and communities to thrive'.[43] Psychology has traditionally been more interested in more negative emotions such as anger, fear and aggression. The best-known works in the field of positive psychology include Martin Seligman's *Learned Optimism* and *Authentic Happiness*; the latter focuses on strengths, values and work. There is the work on optimal mental states – colloquially 'being in the zone' – that is, *Flow* by Mihaly Csikszentmihalyi.[44] In Barbara Frederickson's *broaden-and-build theory* she contends that positive emotions broaden one's awareness and encourage novel, varied and exploratory thoughts and actions. Over time, this expanded behavioural repertoire builds skills and resources. According to Fredrickson, positive emotions build an individual's long-lasting psychological, intellectual, physical and social resources. In short, positive emotional states enable us to tap into a broader, more creative repertoire. When stressed, our focus narrows to typical binary, fight-or-flight survival responses. My approach to confidence building is strongly influenced by Frederickson's theory, and based on two key principles. First, I advocate that confidence begins with relaxation rather than displays of 'peacockery' that aim to dominate. Second, we boost our own confidence as we seek to build confidence in others. Confidence, like gender, is relational. And, rather than a quality gifted to the chosen few (traditionally men), on this view, confidence is based on consensus.[45]

The broaden-and-build theory offers valuable insights for how we advance gender politics – is it through consensus or compliance, the chalice or the blade? Throughout this book, we have touched on human values. These are our drivers and motivations and set the backdrop for our goals, individually and collectively.

Bottom-up and top-down

In novels, fables and films there is often a moral to the story. Beneath the surface entertainment value, lies another level of meaning. On top of this, there is a different construction and interpretation of the stories. One person's mutant with special powers is another person's outsider marginalized because of their differences, that is, LGBTQI+ people.[46]

Gender is a story into which we are born. It is a 'that's just the way things are' narrative. Gender is from the bottom-up and the top-down. It is the social interpretation of biology and a social manifestation of values – the 'natural order'. Biological essentialism, androcentrism and power all operate within a zero-sum game ideology of limited resources. In everyday culture, challenges to this system are ridiculed and people who pose them 'need to be put back in their place', which is often as ominous as it sounds. Consider the tabloid journalism on-going narrative of feminists, that is, 'dour, dungaree-wearing, lentil-eating, men-hating, relics of the 1970s who want to spoil everyone's fun'. This caricature is designed to nullify a whole body of knowledge, experience and understanding that formally began to take shape in the latter decades of the 18th century. Significant improvements have been made in women's rights (and human rights) – in the West – and some might see the battle as largely won. However, advances in rights are fragile in the context of a hierarchical binary system. The period following the banking-instigated financial crash of 2007–2008 had the worst impact on the poorest people, particularly women. People in the UK were told by the government that 'we are all in it together' as the ideology of austerity deployed cuts in services and funding was withdrawn from charities and initiatives supporting the most vulnerable people. It seems that some of us are in 'it' deeper than others. Homophobic attacks increased by 147% in the three months following the Brexit referendum in the UK. It is notable that the maximum prison sentence for an attack on an LGBT person is a quarter of the sentence for racist attacks (six months as opposed to two years) – which have also increased. Gains in equality and changes in attitude can be transitory in uncertain economic and political times.

Pioneering feminist and self-confessed 'devil's advocate' Germaine Greer argues that equality is rather a conservative goal. Ultimately, equality means equal with men, and this overlooks that much of the binary system is not good for all men either. For Greer, liberation from an oppressive system should be the goal.[47] There are parallels

with feminist critiques of mainstream psychology and how unsuc-
cessful tweaks gave way to radical rethinks. In her provocative book
The Whole Woman, Greer argues 'Liberation struggles are not about
assimilation but about asserting difference, endowing that difference
with dignity and prestige and insisting on it as a condition of self-
definition and self-determination'. It's difficult to argue with this aim,
although Greer makes it easier. Her views are often not conducive to
sound-bite media culture and are often out-of-step with prevailing
intersectional feminist thought, that is, we need to consider overlapping
social identities (ethnicity, age, sexuality, class, disability and so on)
and systems of oppression. Greer's views about trans women led to
calls for her to be 'no-platformed', even though her talk *Women & Power:
The Lessons of the 20th Century* did not address trans issues.[48] The dispute
is one of definition, and Greer refuses to accept that the definition of
'real women' should include trans women, and for some (in a very
binary way) this nullifies everything she utters or writes.[49] Genderqueer writers such as trans activist Kate Bornstein also question
whether there is any such thing as 'real' men or 'real' women. They
argue that we should not shy away from asking difficult questions
around gender identity, such as the question of how people who
transition gain, retain or lose privilege or patriarchal dividend in a
hierarchical system.[50] We also need to ask the question of who has
the power to sanction or silence debates around gender. Using a blade
to cut out what you perceive to be a poison chalice is still using the
blade. It is useful to consider the five questions about power and
democracy from British politician Tony Benn:[51] What power have you
got? Where did you get it from? In whose interests do you use it? To
whom are you accountable? How do we get rid of you? These questions apply to anyone who exerts power over the rights and bodies
of others, including those given a platform for their views and those
who attempt to no-platform them. One of the main issues facing
the intersectional perspective is that there are so many interacting
binaries (of privilege) that make it hard to decide where any one
fits into the theorized hierarchical power pyramid. It's a zero-sum,
limited-resource system, and the concrete realities of people's lives

can sometimes get lost in abstract pontifications. The challenge is, in moving forward, how to balance the rights and freedoms of one identity group without it being perceived (or experienced) by other identities as a loss to theirs.

Several writers argue for analysis of gender politics that is more far-reaching. Connell and Pearse advance the arguments that gender has a social and relational impact that extends nationally and internationally, to economies and states, and global relations. They also argue that the impacts of environmental change are unevenly gendered, as women are over-represented amongst people living in poverty.[52] In *The First Sex*, feminist scholar Elizabeth Gould Davis argues that masculine power was the driving force behind environmental pollution. This argument resonates with Riane Eisler's notion of applying principles of partnership-consensus building in our intimate relationships. In the 1970s E. F. Schumacher wrote *Small Is Beautiful: A Study of Economics As if People Mattered*. More than 40 years on and his ideas are still being discussed and debated. Challenging the androcentric 'bigger is better' approach, he argues for a more humane, more dignified, more democratic system, one that uses creativity and one that is less wasteful. Schumacher's philosophy is based on 'enoughness' (chalice) as opposed to 'never-enoughness' (blade). Gender activist Kate Bornstein is perhaps a little too enthusiastic for some, proclaiming in the subtitle of *My Gender Workbook*, a 'Step-by-Step Guide to Achieving World Peace Through Gender Anarchy and Sex Positivity'. This suggests that rather than a 'bit of tinkering around the edges' we need a radical rethink of the system and our goals and values.

One study in the 1990s argued that our way forward is to create a new agenda for the emerging generations – at the time, 18- to 34-year-olds.[53] Reviewing the study's conclusions, what might they think now?

- *Examine values to redefine the balance between the rights, freedoms of men and women* – this has now broadened to include other genders and other identities.

- *Develop strategies which embrace diversity as well as guaranteeing rights* – this is a key challenge for intersectionality in a zero-sum game system.
- *Rethink gender roles in the context of the new economic climate and new patterns of employment and occupation* – or question whether we need gender roles at all, or how many gender roles there might be.
- *Provide more support structures to help people balance their wants, needs and responsibilities – to work, to care for others and to lead fulfilling lives* – however since the financial crisis of 2007–2008, and the austerity agenda, it is not clear within prevailing systems that any of this will be a high priority. As cognitive scientist and political commentator Noam Chomsky argues, 'The West doesn't have to pretend anymore that it's interested in helping anybody'.[54]

Noam Chomsky has a standard response when asked 'what should we do about . . .?' Such as, 'What should we do about terrorism?' or 'What should we do about fake news?' His answer is short and to the point: 'Stop contributing to it'.

We use language to cut up the continua of human experience into simpler, more meaningful units, to create crisp sets,[55] such as man and woman, masculine and feminine, trans and cis, straight and gay. We edit out the middle. We then use language to stitch these units back together to give a sense of a relationship between them. It's a story we have told for a very long time.

So, what can we do about this story?

Stop telling it.

Stop contributing to it.

STORIES OF KNOWLEDGE AND POWER

This final section offers some thoughts and questions to tease out the dynamics of knowledge and power, and gender and power.

In *A Guide for the Perplexed*, economist E. F. Schumacher[56] identifies four fields of knowledge for the individual that might be applied to gender identity. The four fields arise from combining two pairs: myself/the world and outer appearance/inner experience.

1 **I → inner:** self-awareness, that is, of your feelings, thoughts and our selective attention, where we consciously direct our attention.

2 **I → other persons (inner):** awareness of what other people are thinking and feeling, and being able to 'put yourself in their shoes', even if you do not agree with them, that is, empathy. Understanding others is dependent on first developing self-awareness.

3 **Other persons → I:** understanding yourself as an objective phenomenon, that is, how others view you. Knowledge of people, in general, from the fourth way is useful here. Focusing only on the views of others can make you feel insignificant (and powerless), whereas overly focusing on one's self-awareness can make you feel as if you are the centre of the universe. To achieve balance, you need both.

4 **I → the world:** the scientific study of behaviour of the outside world, that's psychology, sociology, anthropology and so on.

Schumacher notes that we only have direct access to fields one (self-awareness) and four (study of the outside world), and only when all four fields of knowledge are nurtured can we have truly unified knowledge. It is the balance between appearances and meaning and purpose. Evidence around gender differences needs to be weighed-up in the light of what we know about the psychological processes by which we simplify a complex environment and make sense of the world. It should also include knowledge of human cognitive development. This, if nothing else, should make us cautious of jumping to black-and-white conclusions or trying to carve-up continua into binaries. Using these four fields of knowledge also highlights the difference between knowing and believing. In a post-truth, emotional view of the world, should personal feelings and access to the Internet trump empirical evidence?

Stainton-Rogers and Stainton-Rogers[57] offer a series of questions to explore the context of what constitutes knowledge and its relationship with power:

1 Whose knowledge is it? Who made it?
2 Why has it been made this way? Whose interests is it serving?
3 Who benefits from it and who loses?
4 What happens because of it? And what would happen if different knowledge were accepted?

And the final word goes to Raewyn Connell and Rebecca Pearse who contend

> gender analysis is work for many hands. It requires the capacity to listen carefully. It requires ways of giving recognition without falling into separatism . . . knowledge about gender has to be considered again and again, in the light of the changing gender dynamics that appear in world politics. Given this willingness to learn, we are convinced that gender theory and research can play a significant role in making a more democratic world.[58]

CONCLUSIONS

The future of the psychology of gender resides in human creativity and how we can bring that to bear on changing interpersonal dynamics. We have considered how different stories have shaped our view of gender and how retelling those stories can reshape it. A new psychology of gender will also reappraise human qualities and traits in non-gendered terms (weeding out personal, social, and psychological biases) and consider other ways of being and doing beyond the hierarchical, androcentric view.

The conclusion to the book that follows draws together the themes, revisits the question it set out to answer and invites you to contemplate the personal impact of the material on your view of your gender.

6

CONCLUSIONS

Moving forward – meaningful gender

To paraphrase Oscar Wilde, 'All [gender] is at once surface and symbol. Those who go beneath the surface do so at their peril'.[1]

When 'doing things by the book', it makes a big difference which book we use. Is it a self-help book, a textbook, a history book, the 'Good Book', a science fiction novel or a book of fairy tales? They all offer radically different world views. Everyday understanding of gender doesn't even acknowledge that we need a book – maybe just a few glossy magazines will do.

Questioning gender is not easy, mainly because so much of it hides in plain sight. Many people never question it at all – why can't we just leave well enough alone? Some people question it all their lives. Gender has its own oral (and visual) tradition where the rights and the wrongs are passed down because 'that's just the way things are'. It becomes a self-serving, closed loop where everything above the surface becomes its own justification. If you doubt this, visit a greeting card shop, or the card aisle at a supermarket. Gender stereotypes are big business. Vast stretches of pink or blue cards to mark each milestone from the cradle to the grave. We send cards to parents proclaiming, 'it's a girl' or 'it's a boy', as if they did not know. Updates each year remind people of their gender, with images of shoes and handbags or sport and bottles of beer, as if they are likely to forget.

Even the flowers at your funeral will be gender appropriate. Heaven forbid that you should 'push up the *wrong* colour daisies'.

The overarching aim of *The Psychology of Gender* has been to offer an invitation to look below the surface, reflect on the hidden assumptions and reappraise how the binary gender system works for you, and how it doesn't. Nothing presented here is intended to undermine anyone's sense of self or shake the foundations of anyone's world. We are pretty much enrolled into one of two mutually exclusive 'private-members' clubs, without knowing what we are getting ourselves into. Unquestionably, this book was written to shake things up – to cast a critical eye over the gender-club rule book. It highlights some of the issues with which we must contend. It is also a reminder that gender can be fun. For some this is a welcome invitation, and for others, it is a step too far. Change is inevitable. Fun is not mandatory.

We began with a lot of questions. Such as, why are AI helper applications feminized? The common-sense view is because females are supposed to be significantly more helpful, whereas the research indicates otherwise. Why are sports segregated on gender lines, when, with the crossover, they could be organized according to body size? Is this just to protect the masculine ego? We are drawn to binary categories as a way of simplifying the world. The down side is that our tendency to view the world as in-groups and out-groups leads to inequalities. So, is the 'different but equal view' ambitious enough? Can we realistically liberate ourselves from the old system? What about a new system, a new paradigm? What might that look like and what might be its impact? Can a change in gender system change the world? Pop-psychology self-help books decree that the system is inevitable. So, should we just laugh at life's absurdities and uphold the status quo? Are we locked irrevocably in a zero-sum game? Are you being held hostage by gender-role stereotypes?

In personal and professional development coaching I work with clients to support them to move forward with their goals, in a personally meaningful way. This often involves a complete life audit to take account of strengths, weaknesses, opportunities and threats. We emphasize the strengths and maximize opportunities and aim to manage weaknesses and re-appraise threats.[2] As gender impacts on everyone, it is not immune to the process. Much like this book, coaching deals with a lot of 'what ifs' and 'maybes'. In helping clients break down limitations and consider a broader range of options, I frame a lot of my questions as appeals to their imagination. Maybe you've read this book just out of curiosity, maybe for an academic assignment,[3] maybe to answer some questions about your own gender or to help someone else answer questions about theirs. Maybe this is just a springboard to further exploration, or maybe you feel you have more than enough information. Maybe nothing has changed. Maybe you will question the relevance next time you are asked to declare your gender. That's a lot of maybes. And that's the point. 'Maybes' are options.

Gender is about both being and belonging. It is a personal identity and a relationship to the social world. Therefore, as notions of gender change, so we must reappraise, renegotiate and reassert our place in it and our relationship to other people who also might be doing the same.[4] Your gender has impact. A new paradigm of gender becomes more than black and white, right and wrong, winners and losers. A new psychology of gender resides in the shades of ambiguity that weren't predicted for us, by others, at the moment of our birth. It's a dynamic, collaborative process of sense making.

As if you haven't had enough questions already, let's finish off with a few more to help you tell your story, paraphrased from Kate Bornstein:[5]

> Knowing what you know now, and knowing yourself as you do, what is your gender? How much say have you had in it? Is there anything about your gender role that 'gets in the way'? What are you denied because of your gender? What are its benefits? When you think of a gender other than yours, what three things do you find most appealing? What would happen if you incorporated those things into your gender role? What would your gender be then? What might be the impact on your life and goals, on other people, on society, the world and so on? What are the questions you want answered?

Keep asking, keep talking to each other and keep listening.
Happy Birthday.

P.S.

In true magazine quiz style, having considered the contents of this book, what will you do next?

1 Do something different
2 Carry on regardless
3 Think about it
4 Finish writing my essay
5 Read something else[6]
6 Check out all the endnotes in this book
7 All of the above

FURTHER READING

BOOKS

Basow, S. A. (1992). *Gender Stereotypes and Roles*, 3rd edition. Pacific Grove: Brooks/Cole.

Bornstein, K. (2013). *My New Gender Workbook: A Step-by-Step Guide to Achieving World Peace Through Gender Anarchy and Sex Positivity*. London: Routledge.

Bornstein, K. (2016). *Gender Outlaw: On Men, Women, and the Rest of Us*. London: Vintage.

Brannon, L. (2017). *Gender: Psychological Perspectives*, 7th edition. London: Routledge.

Burr, V. (1998). *Gender and Social Psychology*. London: Routledge.

Cameron, D. (2007). *The Myth of Mars and Venus*. Oxford: Oxford University Press.

Connell, R. and Pearse, R. (2015). *Gender: In World Perspective*, 3rd edition. Cambridge: Polity Press.

Criado-Perez, C. (2016). *Do It Like a Woman . . . Change the World*. London: Portabello Books.

Eckert, P. and McConnell-Ginet, S. (2013). *Language and Gender*, 2nd edition. Cambridge University Press.

Eisler, R. (1989). *The Chalice and the Blade*. New York: HarperCollins.

Fine, C. (2010). *Delusions of Gender: The Real Science Behind Sex Differences*. London: Icon Books.

Greer, G. (2006). *The Female Eunuch* (Harper Perennial Modern Classics). London: Harper Perennial.

Killerman, S. (2017). *A Guide to Gender: The Social Justice Advocates Handbook*, 2nd edition. Texas: Impetus Books.

Rottblatt, M. (1996). *Apartheid of Sex: Manifesto on the Freedom of Gender*. London: Pandora.

Stainton-Rogers, W. and Stainton-Rogers, R. (2001). *The Psychology of Gender and Sexuality*. Buckingham: Open University Press.

Sycamore, M. N. (2006). *Nobody Passes: Rejecting the Rules of Gender and Conformity*. Emeryville: Seal Press.

Wood, G. W. (2005). *Sex, Lies and Stereotypes, Challenging Views of Women, Men and Relationships*. London: New Holland.

FILMS

For a list of films containing gender-questioning themes (of varying quality) see: www.allmovie.com/characteristic/theme/gender-bending-d1407

Pleasantville (1998). Directed by Gary Ross.

SCIENCE FICTION

Suggested by Wendy and Rex Stainton-Rogers (2001):

Delaney, S. R. (1996). *Trouble on Triton: An Ambiguous Heterotopia*. Middletown, CT: Wesleyan University Press. Originally published in 1977 as *Triton*.

Elgin, S. H. (2000). *Native Tongue*. New York: The Feminist Press. Originally published in 1984.

Gentle, M. (1996). *Ancient Light*. London: Gollancz. Originally published in 1987.

Gentle, M. (1996). *Golden Witchbreed*. London: Orion. Originally published in 1983.

Le Guin, U. (1981). *The Left Hand of Darkness*. London: Orbit. Originally published in 1969.

Le Guin, U. (1999). The Dispossessed. London: Gollancz. Originally published in 1974.

Piercy, M. (2016). *Woman on the Edge of Time*. New York: Del Rey. Originally published in 1976.

AUTHOR'S WEBSITES

For websites supporting an on-going dialogue surrounding the issues discussed in The Psychology of Gender see:

www.psychologyofgender.org

www.nonbinarygender.org

To enquire about coaching or training around gender issues or personal and professional development issues contact:

info@drgarywood.co.uk

NOTES

CHAPTER 1

1 See Philip K. Dick's 'The Minority Report' short story about predictive policing systems that target and apprehend people *before* they have had the chance to commit a crime.

2 Plummer, K. (1996). Foreword: Gender in Question. In R. Elkins and D. King (eds.), *Blending Genders: Social Aspects of Cross-Dressing and Sex-Changing*. London: Routledge, p. xiii.

3 Burr, V. (1998). *Gender and Social Psychology*. London: Routledge, p. 2.

4 Connell, R. and Pearse, R. (2015). *Gender: In World Perspective*. Cambridge: Polity Press, p. ix.

5 Crawford, M. (1998). 'Mars and Venus': Gender Representations and Their Subversion. In *Proceedings of the International Conference on Discourse and the Social Order*, July, Aston University, Birmingham.

6 LGBTQ = Lesbian, Gay, Bisexual, Trans, Queer. When I and A are added, they refer to 'Intersex' and 'Asexual' or 'Allies'. Q is sometimes for 'questioning'.

7 Rothblatt, M. (1996). *The Apartheid of Sex: A Manifesto on the Freedom of Gender*. London: Pandora.

8 See the British Psychological Society (BPS): www.bps.org.uk. See also the American Psychological Association (APA): www.apa.org/

9 See Rosnow, R. L. (1997). *People Studying People: Artifacts and Ethics in Behavioral Research*. New York: W.H. Freeman & Company.

10 For the purposes of our discussion we remain within our species, within the law and assume all parties concerned are consenting adults.

11 Wood, G. W. (2005). *Sex, Lies and Stereotypes: Challenging Views of Women, Men and Relationships.* London: New Holland.

CHAPTER 2

1 Connell, R. and Pearse, R. (2015). *Gender: In World Perspective.* Cambridge: Polity Press, p. 36.

2 Butler, J. (1990). *Gender Trouble: Feminism and the Subversion of Identity.* London: Routledge, p. 33.

3 Connell and Pearse (2015), p. 36.

4 Bem, S. L. (1993). *The Lenses of Gender: Transforming the Debate on Sexual Inequality.* New Haven: Yale University Press.

5 Bornstein, K. (1997). *My Gender Workbook: How to Become a Real Man, a Real Woman, the Real You, or Something Else Entirely.* London: Routledge.

6 You might also meet the term 'phallocentric' meaning penis-centred.

7 Garfinkel, H. (1967). *Studies in Ethnomethodology.* Cambridge: Polity Press.

8 Mullerian ducts in females and Wolffian ducts in males.

9 The vulva is the outer part of the female genitals, which includes the opening of the vagina (sometimes called the vestibule), the labia majora (outer lips), the labia minora (inner lips) and the clitoris.

10 See also The Internal Clitoris on the Museum of Sex website: www.museum ofsex.com/the-internal-clitoris/ accessed 31/5/2017.

11 Wood, G. W. (2005). *Sex, Lies & Stereotypes: Challenging Views of Women, Men and Relationships.* London: New Holland.

12 See Marcio, J., Jorge, N. and Wexner, S. D. (1997). Anatomy and Physiology of the Rectum and Anus. *European Journal of Surgery*, 16, 723–731, and Morin, J. (1998). *Anal Pleasure and Health: A Guide for Men and Women.* San Francisco: Down There Press. In summary: the anus and the surrounding area contain tactile (touch) sensors, sensory fibres, muscles and a nervous structure shared directly with the genitals. It is not possible to distinguish whether some nerve impulses are anal or genital in origin. For people for whom anal stimulation has no erotic significance, a high degree of sensitivity still exists and irrespective of biological sex or sexual orientation there is an involuntary interaction, during orgasm, between genitals and the anus.

13 Wood, G. W. (2000a). The Achilles Hole: Gender Boundary Maintenance and the Anus. *Psychology of Women Section Review*, 2(2), 26–40; Wood, G. W.

(2000b). *Intolerance on Ambiguity, Gender Stereotypes and Attitudes to Sexuality*. PhD Thesis, The British Library.

14 Rothblatt, M. (1996). *The Apartheid of Sex: A Manifesto on the Freedom of Gender*. London: Pandora; Basow, S. A. (1992). *Gender Stereotypes and Roles*, 3rd edition. Pacific Grove, CA: Brooks/Cole Publishing.

15 Plant, S. (1997). *Zeroes and Ones: Digital Women and the New Technoculture*. New York: Doubleday.

16 Confirmed by Dr Neil Gittoes from Birmingham University, in preparation for my 2005 book *Sex, Lies & Stereotypes: Challenging Views of Women, Men and Relationships*. London: New Holland.

17 See Basow, S. A. (1992). *Gender: Stereotypes and Roles*. Pacific Grove: Brooks/Cole; 'Hormones', LiveStrong.com: www.livestrong.com/sscat/hormones/ accessed 26/10/2017

18 Everything is 'rounded-up' to the nearest integer. We are all approximations.

19 Blackless, M., Charuvastra, A., Derryck, A., Fausto-Sterling, A., Lauzanne, K. and Lee, E. (2000). How Sexually Dimorphic Are We? Review and Synthesis. *American Journal of Human Biology*, 12, 151–166. See also Intersex Society of North America: www.isna.org/faq/frequency accessed 31/5/2017

20 See The UK Intersex Association (UKIA): www.ukia.co.uk/ukia/dsd.html accessed 31/5/2017. Of the 48 people attending (by invitation) the conference, only two were people with intersex conditions.

21 See National Adrenal Diseases Association: www.nadf.us/adrenal-diseases/ congenital-adrenal-hyperplasia-cah/ accessed 31/5/2017

22 'Nature abhors a vacuum' is attributed to Aristotle (384–322 BCE), philosopher and scientist. 'Nature and dichotomy' is from Rothblatt's (1995) *The Apartheid of Sex*.

23 Bem, S. L. (1989). *Genital Knowledge and Gender Constancy in Pre-School Children*, cited in Basow (1992), p. 124.

24 This assumes that there are only two fixed genders.

25 See Basow (1992).

26 Freud had a fondness for Greek mythology.

27 Key name is psychologist Albert Bandura (b. 1925).

28 Key names are psychologist Jean Piaget (1896–1980) and psychologist Lawrence Kohlberg (1927–1987).

29 This doesn't acknowledge that transcending binaries might involve even higher levels of cognitive development.

30 See Bussey and Perry (1982), cited in Basow (1992).

31 To test this out, I'm now listed as 'garygender'. Avowedly not cisgender. Somewhere on the trans/nonbinary continuum between gender-questioning and

genderqueer. From Kate Borstein's provocative *gender aptitude test*, I scored 'gender outlaw'. See Borstein, L. (1998). *My Gender Workbook*. London: Routledge.

32 See: www.transequality.org/issues/resources/transgender-terminology accessed 31/5/2017

33 First International Conference on Transgender Law and Employment Policy (1992) pamphlet. ICTLEP 1992. http://research.cristanwilliams.com/2012/03/19/1992-international-conference-on-transgender-law-and-employment-policy/ accessed 31/5/2017

34 LGBTQQIAPP+ is 'short' for Lesbian, Gay, Bisexual, Trans, Queer, Questioning, Asexual, Pansexual, Polysexual plus, sometimes abbreviated as LGBT or LGBTQ+. See Trans Student Educational Resources: www.transtudent.org/definitions accessed 31/5/2017

35 Bevan, T. (2014). *The Psychobiology of Transsexualism and Transgenderism: A New View Based on Scientific Evidence*. California: Praeger.

36 Bornstein, K. (2016). *Gender Outlaw: On Men, Women and the Rest of Us*. New York: Vintage, p. 85.

37 Connell, R. (2012). *Transsexual Women and Feminist Thought*, cited in Connell and Pearse (2015), p. 108.

38 Bornstein (2016), p. 86.

39 Gender Dysphoria leaflet (PDF) from the American Psychiatric Association.

40 Sam Killerman quoted in Steinmetz, K. (2014). *A Comprehensive Guide to Facebook's New Options for Gender Identity in Time Magazine*. See: http://techland.time.com/2014/02/14/a-comprehensive-guide-to-facebooks-new-options-for-gender-identity/ accessed 31/5/2017

41 See Black, P. (2014). Will 'Cisgender' Survive? *The Atlantic*. See: www.theatlantic.com/entertainment/archive/2014/09/cisgenders-linguistic-uphill-battle/380342/ accessed 28/10/2017

42 That would be a pair of continua, one for non-trans ⟷ trans and another for non-cis ⟷ cis. Yes, it makes things more complicated. Gender is complicated. And, many of the problems associated with gender stem from a Procrustean adherence to binaries.

43 See Marinucci, M. (2010). *Feminism Is Queer: The Intimate Connection Between Queer and Feminist Theory*. London: Zed Books, pp. 125–126.

44 See Scott-Dixon, K. (2009). Public Health, Private Parts: A Feminist Public-Health Approach to Trans Issues. *Hypatia*, 24(3), 33–55.

45 Philosopher Jacques Derrida's (1930–2004) notion of hierarchized binary oppositions. Switching emphasis allows us to ask 'What if trans were the default position and non-trans the exception?'

46 See Costello, C. G. (2015). *Cis Gender, Ipso Gender*. http://trans-fusion.blogspot.
co.uk/2015/06/cis-gender-ipso-gender.html

47 LGBTQ+ Definitions from The Trans Student Educational Resources website.
See: www.transstudent.org/definitions accessed 26/10/2017

48 Sam Killerman quoted in Steinmetz (2014).

49 Sam Killerman quoted in Steinmetz (2014).

50 Sounds like a bad title for a Spaghetti Western! Rubin (1993) cited in Wood,
G. W. (2000b). *Intolerance on Ambiguity, Gender Stereotypes and Attitudes to Sexuality*. PhD
Thesis, The British Library.

51 Butler (1990), p. 17.

52 Warner, M. (2000). *The Trouble with Normal: Sex, Politics and the Ethics of Queer Life*.
Cambridge, MA: Harvard University Press.

53 Kitzinger & Kitzinger (1993) cited in Russo, A. (2001). Taking Back Our
Lives: A Call to Action for the Feminist Movement. London: Routledge.

54 Bornstein, K. (2013). *My New Gender Workbook: A Step-by-Step Guide to Achieving
World Peace Through Gender Anarchy and Sex Positivity*. London: Routledge.

55 See Sell, R. L., Wells, J. A. and Wypij, D. (1995). The Prevalence of Homosexual Behaviour and Attraction in the United States, the United Kingdom
and France: Results of National Population-Based Samples. *Archives of Sexual
Behaviour*, 24, 235–248.

CHAPTER 3

1 Martin and Halverson (1981) cited in Stainton-Rogers, W. and Stainton-
Rogers, R. (2001). *The Psychology of Gender and Sexuality*. Buckingham: Open University Press.

2 A state of flux or uncertainty.

3 Stangor and Ruble (1987) cited in Stainton-Rogers and Stainton-Rogers (2001).

4 Condry and Condry (1976) and Frisch (1977) cited in Gross, R. (1992).
Psychology: The Science of Mind and Behaviour. London: Hodder Arnold.

5 Katz, D. (1960). The Functional Approach to the Study of Attitudes. *Public
Opinion Quarterly*, 24, 163–204.

6 In Wood, G. (2013). *Unlock Your Confidence. Find the Keys to Lasting Change Through
the Confidence-Karma Method*. London: Watkins Publishing Ltd, I assert that relaxation is the basis of confidence.

7 Russell, R. (1959). *The Problems of Philosophy*. Oxford: Oxford University Press.

8 There's a scene in the classic film *The Blues Brothers* where the band, having
had do take any gigs they could get, arrives at a venue and asks, 'What kind

of music do you have here?' The owner replies proudly, 'Both kinds! Country AND Western'. For the whole evening, the band's set comprised repeated renditions of the theme tune from *Rawhide* (1960s cowboy TV series) and Tammy Wynnette's *Stand by Your Man*. Perfect theme tunes for gender stereotypes.

9 Bleys, R. C. (1995). *Geography of Perversion*. London: Continuum International Publishing Group.

10 Ochs, R. and Deihl, M. (1992). Moving Beyond Binary Thinking. In W. Blumenfeld (ed.), *Homophobia: How We All Pay the Price*. Boston: Beacon Press, p. 69.

11 Cited in Wood, G. W. (2000). The Achilles Hole: Gender Boundary Maintenance and the Anus. *Psychology of Women Review*, 2(2), 26–40.

12 Allport, G. (1950). *The Nature of Prejudice*. New York: Basic Books.

13 See Goldstein, E. B. (2011). *Cognitive Psychology: Connecting Mind, Research, and Everyday Experience*. Australia: Wadsworth Cengage Learning.

14 Bigler, R. S. and Liben, L. S. (2007) cited in Fine, C. (2010). *Delusions of Gender: The Real Science Behind Sex Differences*. London: Icon Books.

15 Bakan (1966) and Williams and Best (1990) both cited in Basow, S. A. (1992). *Gender Stereotypes and Roles*, 3rd edition. Pacific Grove: Brooks/Cole, p. 4.

16 Asch (1946) cited in Gross (1992). *Psychology: The Science of Mind and Behaviour*. London: Hodder Arnold.

17 The right-brain versus left-brain stuff is based on research half a century old (e.g. Sperry, R. W. (1968). Hemisphere Deconnection and Unity in Conscious Awareness. *American Psychologist*, 23(10), 723). There is some specialization of function in each of the brain's hemispheres but recent research demonstrates there is not a binary split.

18 Nielsen, J. A., Zielinski, B. A., Ferguson, M. A., Lainhart, J. E., Anderson, J. S. (2013). An Evaluation of the Left-Brain vs. Right-Brain Hypothesis With Resting State Functional Connectivity Magnetic Resonance Imaging. *PLoS ONE*, 8(8), e71275. https://doi.org/10.1371/journal.pone.0071275 accessed 30/6/2017

19 Martin, E. (1991). The Egg and the Sperm: How Science Has Constructed a Romance Based on Stereotypical Male-Female Roles. *Signs*, 16(3), 485–501.

20 This resonates with accounts of dangerous female sexuality – sirens luring hapless mariners to their doom.

21 Welter (1966) cited in Basow, S. A. (1992). *Gender Stereotypes and Roles*, 3rd edition. Pacific Grove: Brooks/Cole.

22 Gray, J. (1995). *Mars and Venus in the Bedroom: A Guide to Lasting Romance and Passion*. New York: Harper Collins, p. 29.

23 See page 158 of Potts, A. (1998). The Science/Fiction of Sex: John Gray's Mars and Venus in the Bedroom. *Sexualities*, 1, 153–173.

24 Greer, G. (2006). *The Female Eunuch*. London: Harper Perennial.

25 Connell, R. and Pearse, R. (2015). *Gender: In World Perspective*. Cambridge: Polity Press.

26 American Sociological Association. (2016, August 21). Sex and Gender More Important than Income in Determining Views on Division of Chores. *Science-Daily*. See: www.sciencedaily.com/releases/2016/08/160821093100.htm accessed 25/10/2017

27 Money, J. (1988). *Gay, Straight and In-Between: The Sexology of Erotic Orientation*. Oxford: Oxford University Press.

28 Brill (1913) cited in Wood (2000).

29 See Stainton-Rogers and Stainton-Rogers (2001), p. 55.

30 See 'Zero and One' from the film *Home of the Brave* (1986). Directed by Laurie Anderson.

31 Wood, G. W. (2005). *Sex, Lies & Stereotypes: Challenging Views of Women, Men and Relationships*. London: New Holland.

32 Wood, G. W. (2000).

33 Weinberg, G. (2003). *Why Men Won't Commit: Getting What You Both Want Without Playing Games*. New York: Atria Books.

34 Wood, G. W. (2005).

35 de Beauvoir, S. (1992). *The Second Sex*. London: Vintage Classics.

36 Bornstein, K. (2013). *My New Gender Workbook*. London: Routledge.

37 Even horoscopes offer greater scope for variability, with 12 personality types as opposed to two.

38 Erikson (1978), Berne (1971) and Rothblatt (1996) cited in Wood (2000), p. 27.

39 'Hopefully' because with any technique it might be subject to human bias and the selection of studies can be agenda-driven, albeit unconsciously.

40 In a nutshell, it's the ratio of the difference between the average scores (means) and the spread of the scores (standard deviation).

41 Cohen (1977) cited in Kristoffer Magnusson's online Interpreting Cohen's d Effect Size an Interactive Visualization. See: http://rpsychologist.com/d3/cohend/ accessed 23/7/2017. The broad groupings are to introduce the concepts and ease discussion. For a more in-depth analysis visit Magnusson's site.

42 Basow (1992) based on Cohen (1969). *Statistical Power Analysis for the Behavioral Sciences*. NY: Academic Press: Small (*d* is less than 0.20), small to moderate

(d is greater than 0.20 but less than 0.40), moderate (d is around 0.50 that is greater than 0.40 but less than 0.60), moderate to large (d is greater than 0.60 but less than 0.80), large (d is greater than 0.80 but less than 1.30), very large (1.30 and above).

43 Hyde, J. S. (2005). The Gender Similarities Hypothesis. *American Psychologist*, 60(6), 581–592.

44 The figures in this section are from Hyde (2005). The 1974 review mentioned in Hyde (2005) is Maccoby and Jacklin's *The Psychology of Sex Differences*. Palo Alto: Stanford University Press.

45 Carothers, B. J., and Reis, H. T. (2013). Men and Women Are From Earth: Examining the Latent Structure of Gender. *Journal of Personality and Social Psychology*, 104(2), 385–407.

46 Joel D., Berman, Z., Tavor, I., Wexler, N., Gaber, O., Stein, Y., . . . Assaf, Y. (2015). Sex Beyond the Genitalia: The Human Brain Mosaic. *PNAS*, 12(50), 15468–15473. See: www.pnas.org/content/112/50/15468 accessed 30/6/2017

47 Rippon, G. (2015). A Welcome Blow to the Myth of Distinct Male and Female Brains. *New Scientist*. See: www.newscientist.com/article/dn28584-a-welcome-blow-to-the-myth-of-distinct-male-and-female-brains/ accessed 30/6/2017

48 Fine (2010).

49 Del Giudice, M., Lippa, R. A., Puts, D. A., Bailey, D. H., Bailey, J. M., Schmitt, D. P. (2016). Joel et al.'s Method Systematically Fails to Detect Large, Consistent Sex Differences. *PNAS*, 113(14), E1965. See: www.pnas.org/content/113/14/E1965.full.pdf accessed 30/6/17

50 Del Giudice, M. (2015). Mosaic Brains? A Methodological Critique of Joel et al. (2015). See: http://cogprints.org/10046/1/Delgiudice_etal_critique_joel_2015.pdf accessed 30/6/2017

51 Borrowing the phrase from psychotherapist Carl Rogers (1902–1987).

52 Cited in Stainton-Rogers and Stainton-Rogers (2001), p. 57.

53 Stainton-Rogers and Stainton-Rogers (2001), pp. 56–57.

54 Fine (2010).

55 Stainton-Rogers and Stainton Rogers (2001), p. 115.

56 I don't propose to give a platform to pseudosceptic sites by offering links. When you happen across a website whose preoccupations are UFOs, psychic abilities and feminism as a conspiracy theory, you'll know you are in

the 'right' place. Always ask yourself the question 'Is there likely to be any information that could change the web author's views?'

CHAPTER 4

1 Health Canada, Health Canada's Gender-Based Analysis Policy (2000) cited in Vlassoff, C. (2007). Gender Differences in Determinants and Consequences of Health and Illness. *Journal of Health, Population and Nutrition*, 25(1), pp. 47–61.

2 Basow, S. A. (1992). *Gender Stereotypes and Roles*, 3rd edition. Pacific Grove: Brooks/Cole.

3 Altman (1997) cited in Brannon, L. (2017). *Gender: Psychological Perspectives*, 7th edition. London: Routledge.

4 Vlassoff (2007).

5 Brannon, L. (2017). *Gender: Psychological Perspectives*, 7th edition. London: Routledge.

6 The World Factbook by Central Intelligence Agency, cited in Brannon (2017).

7 Matthews, D. (2015) Sociology in Nursing 3: How Gender Influences Health Inequalities. *Nursing Times* and Vlassoff (2007).

8 La Greca et al. (1995) and Gafvels and Wandell (2006) cited in Vlassoff (2007).

9 White (2013) cited in Matthews (2015), p. 111, 43, 21–23.

10 Learned helplessness is a psychological / attitudinal state coined by positive psychologist Martin Seligman. His book *Learned Optimism* is well worth a read for anyone experiencing anxiety and depression symptoms.

11 Brannon (2017).

12 *Monty Python and the Holy Grail* (1975), directed by Terry Gilliam and Terry Jones.

13 The epitaph on the gravestone of comedian and writer Spike Milligan (1918–2002) reads (in Irish) 'I told you I was ill'.

14 Carmel (2001) cited in Vlassoff (2007).

15 Basow (1992).

16 Walters (1993) and Valkonen and Martikainen (1995) cited in Vlassoff (2007).

17 Broom (2012) cited in Matthews (2015).

18 Brannon (2017).

19 Travis (2005) and Kent, Patel and Verela (2012) cited in Brannon (2017).

20 Katatrepsis Blog (2012). *Why Does Breast Cancer Research Receive More Research Funding Than Prostate Cancer?* See: https://katatrepsis.com/2012/10/30/why-does-breast-cancer-research-receive-more-research-funding-than-prostate-cancer/ accessed 19/8/2017; see also Carter, A. J. and Nguyen, C. N. (2012). A Comparison of Cancer Burden and Research Spending Reveals Discrepancies in the Distribution of Research Funding. *BMC Public Health*, 17, 12, 526.

21 Boseley, S. (2016). Prostate Cancer Laser Treatment Could Be a Gamechanger for Men. *The Guardian*, 20 December 2016. See: www.theguardian.com/society/2016/dec/20/prostate-cancer-laser-treatment-could-be-game-changer-for-men accessed 15/8/2017

22 Austin et al. (2004), Deheeger et al. (2002), and Kaminski et al. (2004) cited in Vlassoff (2007) and Brannnon (2017).

23 Simpson, M. (1994). *Male Impersonators: Men Performing Masculinity*. London: Cassell.

24 NHS Choices. (2017). *Anabolic Steroid Misuse*. See: www.nhs.uk/conditions/anabolic-steroid-abuse/Pages/Introduction.aspx accessed 14/8/2017

25 Heath, United States, 2014, by National Center for Health Statistics, cited in Brannon (2017).

26 Brannon (2017).

27 Brannon (2017).

28 Malone, L. (2015). Transgender Suicide Attempt Rates Are Staggering. *Vocativ*. See: www.vocativ.com/culture/lgbt/transgender-suicide/ accessed 21/8/2017. See also: https://williamsinstitute.law.ucla.edu/wp-content/uploads/AFSP-Williams-Suicide-Report-Final.pdf accessed 21/8/2017

29 Millett (1977) cited in Stainton-Rogers, W. and Stainton-Rogers, R. (2001). *The Psychology of Gender and Sexuality*. Buckingham: Open University Press.

30 Matthews (2015).

31 *Beautiful Red Dress* by Laurie Anderson from her 1989 album *Strange Angels*. And no, I haven't checked her arithmetic.

32 Rathegeber and Vlassoff (2002) cited in Vlassoff (2007).

33 Connell and Pearse (2015), p. 140.

34 Bornstein, K. (2013). *My New Gender Workbook: A Step-by-Step Guide to Achieving World Peace Through Gender Anarchy and Sex Positivity*. London: Routledge.

35 Connell and Pearse (2015).

36 Baumeister, R. F. (2007). Is There Anything Good About Men? Address given at the meeting of the *American Psychological Association* in *San Francisco*, August 24,

2007. See: www.denisdutton.com/baumeister.htm accessed 24/8/2017, and Connell and Pearse (2015).

37 Baumeister (2007).

38 Connell and Pearse (2015).

39 Baumeister (2007).

40 The Titanic Casualty Figures (and what they mean). See: www.anesi.com/titanic.htm accessed 12/8/2017

41 Baumeister (2007).

42 Connell and Pearse (2015).

43 Home Office and Ministry of Justice (2013). *An Overview of Sexual Offending in England and Wales*. London: Author.

44 Office for Victims of Crime (2014). *Responding to Transgender Victims of Sexual Assault*. See: www.ovc.gov/pubs/forge/sexual_numbers.html accessed 12/8/2017

45 Jewkes, R., Fulu, E., Roselli, T., Garcia-Moreno, C. on behalf of the UN Multi-Country Cross-sectional Study on Men and Violence research team. (2013). Prevalence of and Factors Associated With Non-Partner Rape Perpetration: Findings From the UN Multi-Country Cross-Sectional Study on Men and Violence in Asia and the Pacific. *Lancet Global Health*, 1(4), e208–e218. See: www.thelancet.com/journals/langlo/article/PIIS2214-109X(13)70069-X/fulltext accessed 31/7/2017

46 Lees (1996), Warshaw (1988) and Scully and Marolla (1985), cited in Stainton-Rogers and Stainton-Rogers (2001), p. 235.

47 Stainton-Rogers and Stainton Rogers (2001), p. 239. They also highlight portions of the Moirs' text that are homophobic and deny the existence of bisexuality; see p. 198.

48 Peterson, B. E. and Zurbriggen, E. L. (2010). Gender, Sexuality, and the Authoritarian Personality. *Journal of Personality*, 78(6), 1801–1826.

49 Furnham, A. (2015). The Mind of the Authoritarian. *Psychology Today*. See: www.psychologytoday.com/blog/sideways-view/201502/the-mind-the-authoritarian accessed 13/8/2017

50 Duncan, L., Peterson, B. and Winter, D. (1997). Authoritarianism and Gender Roles: Toward a Psychological Analysis of Hegemonic Relationships. *Personality and Social Psychology Bulletin*, 23(1), 41–49.

51 Gormley, B. and Lopez, F. G. (2010). Authoritarian and Homophobic Attitudes: Gender and Adult Attachment Style Differences. *Journal of Homosexuality*, 57(4), pp. 525–538.

52 *Pleasantville* (1998, directed by Gary Ross), reviewed by Edward Johnson-Ott (1998). See: www.imdb.com/reviews/149/14904.html accessed 31/5/2017

CHAPTER 5

1 Stainton-Rogers, W. and Stainton-Rogers, R. (2001). *The Psychology of Gender and Sexuality*. Buckingham: Open University Press.

2 Connell, R. and Pearse, R. (2015). *Gender: In World Perspective*. Cambridge: Polity Press.

3 Japanese comic books with homoerotic content that have a largely teenage female readership.

4 Mulkay (1985) cited in Stainton-Rogers and Stainton-Rogers (2001), p. 197.

5 Stainton-Rogers and Stainton-Rogers (2001), p. 197.

6 Hoffman, R. J. (1984). Vices, Gods and Virtues: Cosmology as a Mediating Factor in Attitudes to Homosexuality. *Journal of Homosexuality*, 9, 27–44.

7 Scarry, E. (1985). *The Body in Pain: The Making and Unmaking of the World*. Oxford. Oxford University Press, p. 181.

8 Bem (1993), Norton (1997), Nye (1999), Jeffrey-Poulter (1991), Moran (1996), and Spencer (1995), cited in Wood, G. W. (2000b). *Intolerance on Ambiguity, Gender Stereotypes and Attitudes to Sexuality*. PhD Thesis, The British Library.

9 Douglas, M. (1969). *Purity and Danger: Concepts of Pollution and Taboo*. London: Routledge & Kegan Paul.

10 Leviticus chapters 17–26 – so-called because it says 'holy' a lot. It outlines the code of conduct for Israelites as a nation of priests.

11 Hoffman (1984), p. 37.

12 Consider how our view of ancient Egyptian religion is tainted by horror-film mummies. Also, how our word for someone without culture is 'philistine', which means Palestinian.

13 Williams, W. L. (1986). *The Spirit and the Flesh: Sexual Diversity in American Indian Culture*. Boston: Beacon Press. Also, Wood, G. W. (2005). *Sex, Lies & Stereotypes: Challenging Views of Women, Men and Relationships*. London: New Holland, and Hoffman (1984).

14 Douglas (1969).

15 Wood, G. W. (2000a). The Achilles Hole: Gender Boundary Maintenance and the Anus. *Psychology of Women Section Review*, 2(2), 26–40.

16 Bleys, R. C. (1995). *Geography of Perversion*. London: Continuum International Publishing Group.

17 Wood, G. W. (2000).

18 Whenever I hear 'God created Adam and Eve not Adam and Steve', I usually ask 'what about Adam and Yves (St Laurent)?' Then I point out that Adam and Eve were created beings (not born) so didn't have navels. They were also vegetarian (See Genesis 1:29–30). Ironically. Noah, the person tasked with saving the animals from the Great Flood was the first person, in the Bible, given permission to eat them (See Genesis 9 verse 3). Clearly, invoking Adam and Eve as an absolute, unchanging standard, involves selective interpretation.

19 I have changed God to 'the gods' and man to 'humans'. The plurals are in the original text, which I have emphasized.

20 Eat your heart out John Gray.

21 The Adam and Eve Story: Eve Came From Where? See: www.biblicalarchaeol ogy.org/daily/biblical-topics/bible-interpretation/the-adam-and-eve-story-eve-came-from-where/ accessed 17/8/2017

22 The (binary) genital metaphor has probably not escaped your attention.

23 Eisler, R. (2015). Human Possibilities: The Interaction of Biology and Culture. *Interdisciplinary Journal of Partnership Studies*, 1(1). See: http://pubs.lib.umn.edu/cgi/viewcontent.cgi?article=1002&context=ijps accessed 17/8/2017

24 Bettelheim, B. (1976). *The Uses of Enchantment: The Meaning and Importance of Fairy Tales*. London: Penguin Books.

25 Wood, G. (2013). *Unlock Your Confidence*. London: Watkins Books.

26 Stainton-Rogers and Stainton-Rogers (2001).

27 The actors are Michael Fassbender and James McEvoy. For examples, see Archive of Our Own: https://archiveofourown.org/. Warning: Some of these are very graphic and include references to sexual violence.

28 Stainton-Rogers and Stainton-Rogers (2001), Wood (2000).

29 Stainton-Rogers and Stainton-Rogers (2001), p. 147.

30 Connell, R. W. (2005). Masculinities (2nd Edition). Cambridge: Polity Press.

31 Stainton-Rogers and Stainton-Rogers (2001), p. 256.

32 Connell and Pearse (2015), pp. 94–95.

33 Basow (1992), p. 328.

34 Bem (1976), cited in Basow (1992).

35 Rothblatt, M. (1996). *The Apartheid of Sex: A Manifesto on the Freedom of Gender*. London: Pandora, p. 115.

36 Bornstein, K. (2013). *My New Gender Workbook: A Step-by-Step Guide to Achieving World Peace Through Gender Anarchy and Sex Positivity*. London: Routledge.

37 Basow (1992).

38 Connell and Pearse (2015), p. 47.

39 Wood, G. W. (2005).

40 Mayer, J. D., Roberts, R. D., & Barsade, S. (2008). Human Abilities: Emotional Intelligence. *Annual Review of Psychology*, 59, pp. 507–536. See: www.research gate.net/publication/5907081_Human_Abilities_Emotional_Intelligence accessed 17/8/2017

41 Goleman, D. (2004). What Makes a Leader? *Harvard Business Review*. See: https:// hbr.org/2004/01/what-makes-a-leader accessed 17/8/2017

42 Goleman, D. (2016). *Women Leaders Get Results*. See: www.danielgoleman.info/ women-leaders-get-results-the-data/ accessed 18/8/2017

43 Definition from Positive Psychology Center Homepage. See: https://ppc.sas. upenn.edu/ accessed 18/8/2017

44 Pronounced 'Cheek-Sent-Me-Hi'

45 Wood, G. W. (2013).

46 Granger, K. (2016). Have You Tried . . . Not Being a Mutant? How The X-Men Movies Fight for LGBT Rights. *Movie Pilot*. See: https://moviepilot. com/posts/3988951 accessed 22/8/2017

47 Listening to Greer reminded me of my Marxist economics lecturer at college who professed 'it's not democracy if you can't vote for another system'.

48 Lewis, H. (2015). What the Row Over Banning Germaine Greer Is Really About. *New Statesman*, 27 October 2015. See: www.newstatesman.com/poli tics/feminism/2015/10/what-row-over-banning-germaine-greer-really- about accessed 1/8/2017

49 For this reason she is labelled with the term TERF, often used as a slur, it means *trans-exclusionary radical feminist*.

50 Bornstein, K. (2016). *Gender Outlaw: On Men, Women and the Rest of Us*. New York: Vintage.

51 Nichols, J. (2014). Tony Benn and the Five Essential Questions of Democracy. *The Nation*. See: www.thenation.com/article/tony-benn-and-five-essential- questions-democracy/ accessed 21/8/2017

52 Connell and Pearse (2015).

53 Wilkinson and Mulgan (1995), cited in Stainton-Rogers and Stainton-Rogers (2001).

54 See: https://chomsky.info/commongood01/ accessed 23/8/2017

55 Sibley, D. (1995). *Geographies of Exclusion*. London: Routledge.

56 Schumacher, E. F. (1995). *A Guide for the Perplexed*, New Edition. London: Vintage.

57 Stainton-Rogers and Stainton-Rogers (2001), p. 181.

58 Connell and Pearse (2015), p. 152.

CHAPTER 6

1 From the preface to Wilde's novel *The Picture of Dorian Gray*. Originally referred to art.

2 Wood, G. (2008). *Don't Wait for Your Ship to Come In . . . Swim Out to Meet It. Tools and Techniques for Positive Lasting Change*. Chichester: Capstone.

3 Or at least enthusiastically flicked through it for a few choice quotations.

4 Or people who don't recognize, or feel the need to challenge or change. They are still part of the process and still need to be included.

5 Bornstein, K. (2016). *Gender Outlaw: On Men, Women, and the Rest of Us? (Revised & Updated)*. New York: Vintage Books.

6 See Further Reading.